AVOIDANT ATTACHMENT RECOVERY SOLUTION:

PROVEN STRATEGIES TO BREAK FREE FROM
EMOTIONAL BARRIERS, OVERCOME FEAR OF
INTIMACY, RECLAIM INNER CONFIDENCE, AND
BUILD SECURE, LASTING RELATIONSHIPS

LUZIVETTE MARTINEZ, RN

CONTENTS

INTRODUCTION

Let me share a story. A successful marketing executive, Emma, sits in a bustling café, sipping her coffee. She scrolls through her phone, tuning out the chatter around her. It's her usual break from a hectic day. Despite her professional success, Emma feels an emptiness in her personal life. Her friendships remain surface-level, and her romantic relationships never seem to last. She struggles to open up, even to those closest to her.

Emma's story isn't uncommon. Many people experience the same struggle—living with avoidant attachment.

Avoidant attachment goes beyond simply shying away from relationships. Emotional barriers create distance, even when you long for connection. The fear of intimacy makes trust feel unattainable. You may find yourself pulling away, building walls instead of bridges. Over time, this pattern can lead to loneliness and a deep sense of being misunderstood.

I know this struggle all too well because I've lived it. I experience avoidant attachment firsthand and understand how it feels like a constant battle—wanting connection yet fearing it. Growing up, I learned to depend on myself, building emotional barriers as a way to shield myself from pain. I know what it's like to feel torn—longing for intimacy but retreating the moment it gets too close.

My name is Luzivette Martinez. As a registered nurse and manager in diverse healthcare settings, I've encountered countless individuals like Emma. I have seen how attachment styles shape both personal and professional relationships. My own experience with avoidant attachment, combined with my professional insights, has deepened my understanding of human connections and reinforced the importance of recognizing how our attachment styles influence our lives.

I understand—breaking free from avoidant attachment can feel overwhelming. But there is hope. Through my own journey and the stories of others, I've learned that healing is possible. In this book, I aim to provide practical, science-backed strategies that are simple to apply in everyday life. You'll find real stories from people who have walked this path, offering a sense of solidarity and support as you work toward change.

The purpose of this book is straightforward yet impactful: to guide you on a journey of self-discovery and healing from avoidant attachment. You'll learn how to build secure, lasting relationships without losing your sense of self. What makes this book different is its emphasis on real-life application and genuine understanding. This isn't just a theoretical discussion—it's a practical guide to meaningful change.

The book is designed to take you from awareness to action. We'll begin by uncovering the roots of avoidant attachment, exploring how these patterns form. From there, we'll shift to actionable strategies for transformation. Key chapters focus on building trust, embracing vulnerability, and setting healthy boundaries. Each section provides practical tools to support real, lasting progress.

Throughout the book, you'll find language and examples that resonate with your experiences. Whether you're facing challenges in the workplace, navigating family dynamics, or striving for personal growth, this book offers insights that are both relatable and action-able. We address struggles such as difficulty trusting others, the need for complete self-reliance, and hesitation to show vulnerability. With clear, practical strategies, you'll gain the confidence to overcome these barriers and cultivate deeper, more fulfilling relationships in every area of your life.

I invite you to commit to this journey of transformation. Change isn't easy, but the rewards are life-changing. Imagine breaking free from the cycle of avoidant attachment and stepping into secure, fulfilling relationships. This book will guide you through that process.

As you read, remember that patience and persistence are essential. The strategies outlined here take time and effort, but with dedication, you can shift your attachment style and transform your relationships.

Finally, let's talk about hope. Healing and meaningful connections aren't just distant possibilities—they are real, achievable goals. With the right tools and mindset, you can break old patterns and build relationships that bring genuine fulfillment. So, let's begin this journey together. A future of secure, lasting relationships starts now.

1

UNDERSTANDING AVOIDANT ATTACHMENT

There comes a moment in life when we recognize that something about our emotional patterns feels off. You might be at a friend's wedding, watching them exchange vows, and instead of feeling pure joy, a sense of detachment lingers. A part of you wants to celebrate, to fully join in the festivities, but another part holds back. It's as if an invisible barrier stands between you and the rest of the world. Often, this quiet resistance is the subtle signal of avoidant attachment—a pattern that can shape our relationships, distancing us from the warmth and connection we deeply long for.

The Origins of Avoidant Attachment

Attachment theory, a fundamental framework for understanding human relationships, was introduced by John Bowlby and later expanded by Mary Ainsworth. Bowlby, a British psychologist, studied the deep distress infants experience when separated from their parents, proposing that early bonds are essential to emotional development. His research suggested that a child's sense of security—or lack thereof—stems from the responsiveness of their caregiver. Ainsworth, an American-Canadian developmental psychologist, built upon Bowlby's work with her well-known Strange Situation experiment. Through this research, she identified different attachment styles, including secure, avoidant, and anxious. Secure attachment is evident when a child becomes distressed upon a caregiver's departure but is comforted by their return. In contrast, avoidant attachment manifests as emotional detachment, where a child appears indifferent to both the caregiver's absence and return. These foundational insights reveal how attachment styles extend into adulthood, shaping our emotional responses and influencing the way we connect with others.

In early childhood, a child's world centers around their caregivers. When these primary figures are emotionally or physically unavailable, children often adapt by minimizing their emotional expression. Imagine a toddler reaching out for comfort and finding none. Over time, they learn to suppress their needs and emotions to shield themselves from disappointment. This lack of responsiveness from caregivers lays the foundation for avoidant attachment. Emotional availability—or the absence of it—plays a crucial role. When a caregiver is consistently unresponsive, children become self-reliant, developing a perceived independence that often masks their deeper need for connection and support.

Beyond individual interactions, environmental and genetic factors also shape avoidant attachment. Family dynamics, such as an emotionally distant household, reinforce avoidant behaviors. Some individuals may also have a genetic predisposition that heightens their susceptibility to this attachment style. Additionally, past experiences, including trauma or chronic stress, can intensify these tendencies. A child raised in an environment where emotional expression is neither encouraged nor acknowledged may withdraw emotionally as a means of self-preservation. Over time, this learned response can define their approach to relationships, making it difficult to establish close, supportive bonds.

The lasting impact of early attachment experiences is significant. Individuals with avoidant attachment often struggle to build deep, meaningful relationships. The early lessons of self-reliance and emotional suppression can become obstacles to intimacy later in life. These patterns may lead to difficulty regulating emotions, creating a disconnect between outward composure and inner turmoil. The inability to express feelings can strain relationships, leaving partners feeling shut out or unappreciated. This emotional reserve can also affect friendships and professional interactions, fostering cycles of misunderstanding and isolation. The challenge lies in recognizing these patterns and actively working to bridge the gap between past experiences and the present need for connection.

Case Study: Emma's Story

Emma's parents failed to provide emotional support during her childhood. Her father frequently traveled for business, and her mother, absorbed in her own struggles, remained emotionally distant. Early on, Emma learned that expressing her needs often led to disappointment. As an adult, she finds it difficult to rely on others, choosing instead to keep her emotions tightly guarded. While she excels in her career, she struggles with close relationships and often feels overwhelmed by the demands of intimacy. Emma's story is a powerful example of how early attachment experiences shape our interactions later in life. Recognizing these patterns is essential to breaking unhealthy cycles and building healthier, more fulfilling relationships.

My story is much like Emma's. When I was five, my parents sat my brother—who was nearly seven—and me down to tell us they were getting a divorce. We were devastated. My father was a great dad and a loving husband, so I couldn't understand why he was leaving us. I felt abandoned and confused, and those feelings deepened when I later learned he had moved into a new apartment with another woman.As a child, this discovery left me with a profound sense of rejection. I began to believe that the people I loved could leave me without explanation. Meanwhile, my mother, now raising us alone, worked tirelessly to provide for us. She juggled long hours while carrying the full weight of both parent and provider. Her determination ensured we had what we needed, but emotional support sometimes took a backseat as she focused on survival.

These early experiences planted the roots of avoidant attachment in my life, leading me to protect myself by withdrawing emotionally and keeping my feelings locked away. I learned to rely solely on myself, building barriers to shield against the pain of loss and rejection.

Recognizing where avoidant attachment begins is the first step in understanding its impact on your life. Gaining insight into how this attachment style develops allows you to break free from patterns of emotional withdrawal and create a foundation for secure, meaningful connections. When we examine the root causes of our attachment struggles—as I've done in my own journey—we begin to see these patterns more clearly and take the necessary steps toward healing.

How Avoidant Attachment Shapes Adult Relationships

In romantic relationships, avoidant attachment often dictates the unspoken rhythm between partners. One person may feel as if they are teetering on the edge of intimacy—drawn toward connection yet paralyzed by the fear of losing themselves in it. The fear of closeness and dependency leads many to create emotional distance, keeping their partners at arm's length. This isn't a conscious decision but a learned response, a defense mechanism developed over time.The paradox of craving connection while fearing vulnerability fuels a push-pull dynamic that can leave both partners feeling confused and emotionally drained. Emotional withdrawal becomes second nature, an instinctive retreat when the relationship calls for openness or when emotions intensify. This distancing isn't rooted in indifference but in a deeply ingrained need to maintain a sense of independence.

Communication, the lifeline of any relationship, often weakens under the strain of avoidant attachment. People with avoidant tendencies frequently sidestep conversations that require vulnerability or involve conflict, leaving unresolved issues to linger. They may resist discussing their feelings or needs, fearing that such openness could expose them to judgment or rejection. When conflicts arise, shutting down becomes a defense mechanism, creating a silent divide between partners. This avoidance fosters misunderstandings, as silence is often misinterpreted as disinterest or indifference. The result is a cycle of unmet needs and growing tensions, where the lack of communication fuels insecurity and doubt.

Trust is another casualty in relationships affected by avoidant attachment. Establishing trust requires openness and emotional availability—areas where avoidant individuals often struggle. A deep-seated belief in self-reliance can make it difficult for them to depend on their partners, hindering the development of a relationship built on mutual support. Expressing vulnerability, which strengthens trust, can feel risky, as if revealing too much could lead to heartbreak. This reluctance creates emotional distance, leaving partners feeling excluded from each other's inner worlds. Over time, the absence of trust erodes the foundation of the relationship, making it harder to withstand life's inevitable challenges.

Avoidant attachment extends beyond romantic relationships, shaping friendships and family dynamics in subtle yet impactful ways. A preference for independence often leads to keeping friendships at a surface level, avoiding deeper emotional connections. While avoidant individuals may thrive in professional or casual social settings where emotional investment is minimal, their tendency to withdraw makes sustaining close friendships difficult. The avoidance of emotional entanglements can create a social circle filled with acquaintances rather than meaningful friendships.

. . .

Within family relationships, this attachment style may manifest as an unwillingness to engage in emotionally charged discussions or gatherings. This reluctance can create a sense of distance, leading family members to perceive them as detached or uninterested. Yet beneath this exterior often lies a longing for connection, masked by the fear of vulnerability and dependence.

Understanding these dynamics is essential for individuals striving to build healthier relationships despite avoidant attachment. Recognizing these patterns serves as a foundation for change, creating opportunities to break down the barriers that hinder emotional intimacy. The path toward stronger, more fulfilling connections begins with acknowledging these challenges and making intentional efforts to embrace openness and trust.

Recognizing Avoidant Patterns in Your Life

Recognizing avoidant patterns in your life can feel like unraveling behaviors that have become second nature. These tendencies often emerge subtly, showing up as a reluctance to commit or a deep-seated sense of emotional detachment. You might hesitate when a relationship starts to deepen, feeling an instinctive urge to withdraw rather than engage. This reaction isn't a lack of desire for connection but a learned response to the vulnerability that intimacy requires. Emotional detachment, on the other hand, can make interactions feel transactional rather than meaningful, as if a part of you remains guarded, ensuring you never fully invest. This distance can leave others feeling shut out, even when you are physically present, creating an invisible but undeniable barrier.

Self-reflection is essential for understanding these avoidant tendencies. Taking time to practice mindfulness can help identify areas where these patterns persist. Mindfulness allows you to observe your thoughts and emotions without judgment, making it easier to recognize your reactions and behaviors for what they truly are. Journaling can enhance this process, acting as a mirror that reflects your internal world. Writing down your thoughts and emotions can reveal patterns and triggers that might otherwise go unnoticed. For instance, you may realize you tend to withdraw in moments of closeness or react defensively to specific phrases. This awareness is the first step in reshaping ingrained behaviors, offering clarity on the fears and motivations that drive them.

Examining your relationship history can provide further insight into these patterns. Consider creating a timeline of significant relationships, noting the dynamics and outcomes of each. Look for recurring themes, such as how conflicts were handled or how relationships ended. This exercise can uncover unconscious scripts that have shaped your interactions—scripts that may have been written long ago but continue to influence your choices. You might notice a pattern of abrupt endings or friendships that never deepened past a certain point. These observations aren't signs of failure but opportunities to understand and reshape the underlying story that guides your relationships.

Interactive Element: Relationship Mapping Exercise

Create a relationship timeline, noting significant moments and their outcomes. Identify recurring themes and reflect on what these patterns reveal about your attachment style.

Another valuable tool in recognizing avoidant tendencies is seeking feedback from those who know you well. Honest conversations with trusted friends or partners can provide perspectives you might otherwise overlook. Approach these discussions with openness, inviting insight into your relational behaviors. Questions like, "When do you notice me pulling away?" or "How do I handle conflict?" can spark revealing and sometimes challenging conversations. These feedback-driven discussions require vulnerability but pave the way for a deeper understanding and stronger connections. This process isn't about inviting criticism but about gathering meaningful insights that support your growth. It's a collaborative effort to identify and address patterns that may be holding you back in your relationships.

By doing so, you begin dismantling the protective barriers that have kept you at a distance, making room for healthier and more fulfilling connections. Understanding these patterns isn't about placing blame —it's about gaining clarity. And with clarity comes the power to make intentional choices, shaping relationships based on your desire for connection rather than your fear of it. Recognizing avoidant patterns is the first step toward meaningful transformation—one that has the potential to enrich your life and relationships in ways you may not have imagined.

The Emotional Landscape of Avoidant Attachment

The internal world of someone with avoidant attachment is often a maze of conflicting emotions and desires. At its core lies a deep-seated fear of rejection and abandonment. This fear isn't just a passing worry—it's a persistent anxiety that influences every interaction. When faced with the possibility of closeness, the mind races with what-ifs: What if I open up and they leave? This question lingers in the background, shaping decisions and behaviors.

The desire for autonomy becomes a sanctuary, offering a sense of control. Independence isn't merely a preference—it's a shield against vulnerability, providing security and a retreat from the turmoil of unpredictable emotions. This need for self-sufficiency can sometimes manifest as an intense focus on personal achievements or an overreliance on self-reliance, where success is mistaken for emotional fulfillment.

Individuals with avoidant attachment often develop defense mechanisms to cope with their emotional landscape. One common strategy is emotional distancing—keeping emotions at arm's length to minimize the risk of pain. This isn't a sign of indifference but a subconscious effort to maintain stability. Another tactic is rationalization. By intellectualizing emotions, they construct a logical framework that feels safer and easier to manage. It's not that I don't care; I just prefer my own company becomes a repeated internal mantra. While these strategies serve as protective measures, they can eventually become barriers to genuine connection, creating an emotional divide that widens over time.

Self-perception and self-esteem often suffer in the process. The ongoing effort to avoid vulnerability can lead to a persistent sense of unworthiness. A recurring inner voice whispers, You are not enough, whenever intimacy presents itself. Over time, this self-doubt erodes confidence, making it difficult to believe in one's value in relationships. As a result, achievements and external validation may become the sole measures of self-worth. Without emotional connections to reinforce their sense of being lovable and deserving, individuals may struggle to recognize their intrinsic value.

Managing emotional triggers is a critical skill for those with avoidant attachment. The first step is identifying these triggers. A specific phrase, a particular setting, or an unexpected interaction can activate the instinct to withdraw. Keeping a journal to track emotional reactions can help map out recurring patterns. Awareness plays a pivotal role in change. Once triggers are identified, emotional regulation techniques can be applied to manage them effectively. Strategies such as deep breathing, mindfulness, or cognitive reframing help counteract the immediate urge to disconnect. Strengthening these skills over time leads to greater emotional stability, allowing for more thoughtful responses rather than reactive withdrawal.

The emotional experience of avoidant attachment is complex and challenging, but it is not unchangeable. By gaining a deeper understanding of these internal patterns and the defenses at play, individuals can begin to approach their emotions with greater awareness and purpose. This process requires peeling back layers of learned behaviors and fears to uncover the possibility of genuine connection and self-acceptance. It's about recognizing that while these patterns once served as protection, they no longer have to dictate future relationships. Instead, there is space to embrace a new narrative—one that welcomes vulnerability, trust, and deeper, more meaningful connections.

Debunking Myths About Avoidant Attachment

Avoidant attachment is often misunderstood, with many misconceptions distorting how it is perceived. One of the most common myths is that individuals with avoidant tendencies are emotionally cold. People frequently mistake emotional detachment for a lack of feeling or empathy. I know this firsthand—my friends, family, and husband often tell me I seem distant or indifferent. However, the reality is far more complex. Those with avoidant attachment, myself included, are not devoid of emotions; we simply process and express them differently. While my exterior may appear calm and composed, beneath the surface lies a deeply emotional world shaped by past experiences and self-preservation strategies. Recognizing that this detachment is a defense mechanism rather than a rejection of others can encourage greater understanding and patience.

Another widespread misconception is equating independence with emotional strength or well-being. While independence is often valued in many cultures, for individuals with avoidant attachment, it can serve as a barrier to vulnerability. I understand this all too well—I tend to do everything myself, as if no one else can do it as well as I can. But this behavior doesn't stem from arrogance; it is rooted in a deeply ingrained fear of relying on others. For those with avoidant tendencies, independence isn't about self-sufficiency—it's about minimizing the risk of disappointment or rejection. The challenge lies in distinguishing between healthy autonomy and the isolation that avoidant behaviors can create. This emotional distancing can lead to misunderstandings in relationships, where partners, friends, or family members may perceive it as a lack of interest or commitment when, in reality, it is a protective response to perceived threats to personal space and emotional security.

To fully understand avoidant attachment, it is essential to compare it with other attachment styles, such as anxious attachment. While individuals with avoidant attachment may withdraw from closeness, those with anxious attachment often seek it intensely, fearing abandonment. This contrast highlights how different people cope with the same core fears of rejection and loss. I explored these dynamics in greater depth in my other book, *Anxious Attachment Recovery Solution,* where I examine the struggles of those with anxious attachment and offer practical tools for healing.

In contrast, secure attachment represents a balance—where individuals feel comfortable with both intimacy and independence. People with secure attachment navigate relational challenges with emotional openness and trust, allowing them to build healthy personal and professional relationships. Their adaptability demonstrates how understanding attachment patterns can lead to meaningful growth and stronger connections.

Recognizing these contrasts helps you identify your own attachment style while also fostering empathy for others. By becoming aware of these patterns, you can work toward building more secure relationships and improving your interactions in all areas of life.

Despite its challenges, avoidant attachment also has notable strengths. Independence and self-reliance can be valuable in various aspects of life, helping individuals excel in situations that require autonomy and self-direction. The ability to self-soothe is another advantage, enabling them to manage stress without relying on external validation or support. When balanced with emotional openness, these qualities contribute to a well-rounded and resilient personality.

Encouraging inclusive perspectives is crucial for understanding the complexities of avoidant attachment. Cultural influences play a significant role in shaping attachment behaviors. In some cultures, emotional restraint and self-sufficiency are highly valued, reinforcing avoidant tendencies. Acknowledging these cultural factors allows for a more compassionate understanding of why certain behaviors develop and how they can be addressed. Additionally, diverse relationship dynamics emphasize that there is no one-size-fits-all approach to navigating or overcoming avoidant attachment. Every individual's experiences and background influence their attachment style, requiring personalized approaches to support and intervention.

As we conclude this discussion, it is important to recognize that avoidant attachment is not an unchangeable barrier but a pattern that can be understood and transformed. By dispelling myths and acknowledging the strengths within this attachment style, we create opportunities for more compassionate interactions and deeper self-awareness. This understanding encourages a more inclusive view of relationships, where emotional diversity is embraced rather than judged. Moving forward, let this awareness guide our interactions—offering empathy, patience, and encouragement to those working through the complexities of avoidant attachment while fostering positive growth in our relational experiences.

2

SELF-DISCOVERY AND EMOTIONAL AWARENESS

I magine standing at the edge of a dense forest, a path before you shrouded in shadows. You hesitate, uncertain of what lies ahead, yet drawn by the promise of discovery. This is the essence of self-discovery—a journey inward, filled with uncertainty yet rich in possibility. In today's fast-paced world, introspection is often dismissed as a luxury rather than recognized as a necessity. However, understanding yourself is fundamental to personal growth and building meaningful relationships. It requires peeling away layers to uncover your true self, recognizing what drives you, and understanding how your values and beliefs influence your choices.

Self-awareness is the foundation of personal development, offering valuable insight into your inner world and its impact on your interactions. Taking time for introspection allows you to identify the core values and beliefs that shape your decisions. This process involves reflection, questioning assumptions, and uncovering truths buried under societal expectations or past experiences. Gaining this awareness helps align your actions with your authentic self, leading to a deeper sense of purpose and integrity.

Various methods can aid in the exploration of self-awareness and personal growth, each providing a unique lens for understanding yourself.

Personality assessments, such as the Myers-Briggs Type Indicator (MBTI) and the Enneagram, offer structured frameworks for recognizing your natural tendencies. The MBTI categorizes personalities into 16 types based on factors like introversion versus extraversion and thinking versus feeling, helping you understand how you engage with the world and make decisions. Meanwhile, the Enneagram outlines nine interconnected personality types, focusing on core motivations and fears. These assessments reveal underlying behavioral patterns, offering a roadmap for self-reflection and personal evolution.

Creative expression is another powerful tool for self-exploration. Engaging in activities like painting, writing, or playing music allows you to channel emotions and thoughts that may be difficult to verbalize. Art taps into the subconscious, uncovering insights beyond words. For example, journaling helps process emotions and track recurring themes, while painting or music provides an outlet for complex feelings that might otherwise remain unspoken.

By integrating these tools—structured assessments and creative practices—you can deepen your understanding of yourself, gain fresh perspectives, and discover effective ways to grow.

Mindfulness is the practice of being fully present and aware of the moment without judgment. It involves observing thoughts, emotions, and bodily sensations with curiosity and acceptance. By cultivating mindfulness, you create space to understand yourself on a deeper level and respond to life's challenges with greater clarity and intention.

Mindful breathing is one of the simplest yet most effective ways to practice mindfulness. By focusing on the rhythm of your breath—how it moves in and out—you can anchor yourself in the present moment. This practice calms the mind, reduces stress, and increases awareness of your thoughts and emotions without feeling over-whelmed.

Another beneficial mindfulness technique is body scan meditation, which involves observing sensations, tension, or discomfort in different areas of the body. This practice strengthens the connection between mind and body, helping you recognize areas that need care and attention.

Through these practices, mindfulness becomes a powerful tool for self-discovery and emotional balance, allowing you to approach life with greater calm, focus, and resilience.

Setting intentions for growth is another essential step in your self-discovery journey. Crafting a personal mission statement can serve as a guiding force, aligning your actions and decisions with your core values and aspirations. It is a declaration of who you are and who you strive to become, offering clarity and direction during uncertain times. Daily affirmations can support this process by reinforcing posi-tive beliefs and strengthening self-awareness. These affirmations serve as gentle reminders of your intentions, keeping you mindful and focused throughout the day.

Interactive Element: Crafting Your Mission Statement

Consider the values and aspirations that matter most to you. Reflect on how they shape your daily life and the person you strive to become. Craft a personal mission statement that captures these reflections, serving as a clear guide for your journey.

As you explore self-discovery and emotional awareness, remember that patience and openness are essential. The insights you gain will deepen your understanding of yourself and strengthen your connections with others. Embracing this process lays the groundwork for a more genuine and fulfilling life.

Building Emotional Intelligence: A Toolkit

Emotional intelligence is the ability to recognize, understand, and manage our own emotions while also being attuned to the feelings of others. This skill is essential for both personal fulfillment and meaningful relationships.

Imagine a day at the office when tensions are high, and a colleague's remark affects you more than expected. Your initial reaction might be defensive or dismissive. However, emotional intelligence allows you to pause, acknowledge your emotions, and identify their source—perhaps stress from an impending deadline or a past misunderstanding with that colleague. This awareness transforms your response, leading to more constructive communication. Instead of reacting defensively, you might ask clarifying questions or express how the comment made you feel, paving the way for mutual understanding and resolution.

Now, consider a personal relationship—perhaps a disagreement with your partner about household responsibilities. Without emotional intelligence, you might focus solely on your frustration, escalating the conflict. However, emotional awareness allows you to pause and consider both your emotions and your partner's perspective. You may realize that their dismissive tone stems from exhaustion after a long day rather than indifference. This understanding enables you to approach the conversation with empathy, validating their feelings while expressing your own needs in a calm, non-confrontational manner.

Emotional intelligence is more than a soft skill—it shapes how we interpret interactions and make decisions that align with our values and goals. It serves as a guiding force, helping us cultivate stronger, more meaningful relationships in both professional and personal settings.

Developing emotional intelligence begins with self-awareness. This involves recognizing your emotional responses and identifying the triggers behind them. One effective strategy is tracking emotions through journaling. By consistently recording your emotional experiences, you start noticing patterns—perhaps you frequently feel anxious during team meetings or become frustrated when discussing certain topics. Identifying these triggers is key to understanding their root causes. With this insight, you can shift from reacting impulsively to choosing your emotional responses with greater intention. Rather than being controlled by emotions, you gain the ability to manage them in a way that aligns with your well-being.

Empathy and social skills are foundational to emotional intelligence, allowing you to connect with others on a deeper level. Strengthening these skills requires conscious effort. Active listening is a powerful tool—fully focusing on the speaker without distractions or judgment fosters deeper understanding and demonstrates respect. Perspective-taking exercises also enhance empathy by encouraging you to see situations from another person's point of view. Imagining what someone else is feeling or experiencing broadens your understanding and strengthens interpersonal connections. These practices create a sense of emotional closeness, reinforcing the bonds that sustain meaningful relationships.

Empathy is the bridge that unites individuals, providing compassion and support when it's needed most. By nurturing emotional intelligence, we develop the ability to communicate with clarity, respond with understanding, and build relationships rooted in trust and mutual respect.

Managing emotions effectively is a key component of emotional intelligence. It requires maintaining emotional balance, particularly in stressful situations. Breathing techniques can be incredibly useful in these moments. When faced with stress, the body reacts instinctively, often intensifying emotions. Practicing controlled breathing helps calm the nervous system, restoring a sense of composure. Techniques such as the 4-7-8 method—inhaling for four seconds, holding for seven, and exhaling for eight—can provide immediate relief.

Another powerful strategy is cognitive reframing, which involves shifting your perception of a situation by replacing negative interpretations with positive or neutral ones. By adjusting your mindset, you gain control over your emotional reactions, reducing stress and improving overall well-being. While emotions are strong influences on behavior, the right tools allow you to manage them effectively, helping you respond thoughtfully rather than impulsively.

Emotional intelligence is not just an inherent trait but a set of skills that can be developed and practiced over time. As you apply these strategies, you'll find yourself handling relationships with greater ease and understanding. Developing emotional intelligence is a personal journey, yet its effects extend far beyond the individual, enriching every connection and interaction in your life.

Self-Reflection: A Path to Understanding

Reflecting on one's life is like holding a mirror up to the soul. In moments of introspection, we gain clarity about our behaviors and emotions. Reflection allows us to pause and examine our thoughts and actions, creating space to understand the reasons behind our reactions. Through regular reflection, you can recognize patterns that might otherwise remain unnoticed. This practice builds self-awareness and serves as a powerful tool for problem-solving. By analyzing past actions and their outcomes, you can determine what works and what doesn't, leading to more informed decisions in the future. Reflection is not just about looking back—it's about learning and growing from the past to shape the present and future.

Journaling provides a structured way to explore thoughts and emotions. It's an opportunity to put pen to paper and let your mind flow freely without judgment. Guided prompts can help direct your thoughts, encouraging you to examine specific areas of your life. Questions like "What am I thankful for today?" or "How did I handle a recent challenge?" offer a starting point for deeper exploration. Reflective writing exercises allow you to articulate feelings and experiences, offering insights that may not come through spoken words. Writing can be cathartic, helping you process emotions and gain a fresh perspective on your life. Over time, these journals become a personal archive of growth, charting your journey through life's complexities.

Incorporating reflective practices into your daily routine can deepen self-awareness. Evening reflection routines, for instance, provide a time to unwind and process the day's events. These moments might involve sitting quietly with a cup of tea, reviewing your interactions, and considering the lessons learned. Retreats or workshops offer a more immersive experience, allowing you to step away from daily distractions and focus entirely on self-examination. These settings create a sense of connection, where sharing insights with others enhances personal growth. Making reflection a regular practice cultivates a habit of continuous self-discovery and understanding.

Despite its benefits, self-reflection can be challenging. The fear of confronting difficult emotions often holds people back from engaging in this practice. It's natural to avoid uncomfortable truths, but doing so only prolongs the discomfort. To ease into reflection, start small. Allow yourself to explore thoughts and feelings gradually, without the pressure to resolve everything at once. Developing a reflective mindset requires patience and self-compassion. Not every session will bring profound revelations, and that's okay. The goal is progress, not perfection. Creating a supportive, nonjudgmental environment can encourage more honest and productive introspection.

Recognizing Emotional Triggers

Imagine you are at a family gathering, and a relative makes an offhand comment about your career choices. Suddenly, you react more intensely than expected, perhaps with anger or defensiveness. These reactions often stem from emotional triggers—stimuli that provoke a strong emotional response. Triggers can be words, situations, or even memories tied to past experiences, bringing unresolved emotions to the surface. They play a significant role in our daily interactions, sometimes catching us off guard. Recognizing these triggers is essential because they often originate from deep-seated vulnerabilities or past wounds. Understanding your triggers strengthens self-awareness and equips you to manage your responses more effectively.

Identifying your unique emotional triggers requires reflection and keen observation. Consider keeping a trigger journal to document instances that elicit strong emotional reactions. Over time, patterns will emerge, revealing the specific situations or comments that consistently provoke a response. For example, you may notice that even constructive criticism stirs feelings of inadequacy, possibly linked to past experiences where you felt undervalued. Analyzing these patterns allows you to draw connections between your current reactions and past experiences. This insight is the first step in turning triggers from sources of distress into opportunities for growth. By gaining clarity on your emotional responses, you build a strong foundation for lasting change.

Once you've identified your triggers, the next step is learning to respond constructively. I've experienced firsthand how difficult this can be. I used to be easily triggered by other people's words or actions, often reacting impulsively. My immediate response was to isolate myself, stewing in anger and frustration. However, this only deepened my emotional turmoil and made it harder to move forward.

I've learned to manage these reactions by practicing grounding techniques, which help de-escalate emotions. Breathing exercises, in particular, have been a turning point for me. When I feel triggered, I take slow, deliberate breaths, focusing on each inhale and exhale to calm my racing thoughts. This simple act of mindfulness helps me stay present and gives me the space to respond thoughtfully rather than react impulsively.

Developing a personal action plan for triggers has also been invaluable. This plan includes strategies like momentarily stepping away from the situation to regain composure, using positive self-talk to challenge negative thoughts, and practicing self-compassion. These proactive measures have empowered me to handle emotional triggers with confidence and resilience, reducing their impact on my daily life and relationships.

By identifying triggers and implementing grounding techniques, you can better handle challenging moments, transforming your reactions into opportunities for growth and self-awareness.

Building resilience to emotional triggers involves strengthening coping mechanisms and practicing emotional detachment. Coping mechanisms are strategies that help you manage stress and difficult emotions. These can include activities like exercise, meditation, or engaging in hobbies that bring you joy. Such practices act as a buffer against emotional distress, allowing you to maintain composure under pressure. Emotional detachment, on the other hand, involves maintaining a healthy distance from your emotions, enabling you to observe them without becoming overwhelmed. It's not about suppressing feelings but acknowledging them without allowing them to dictate your actions. By cultivating this balance, you can navigate emotional challenges with a steady and composed mindset.

Identifying, managing, and building resilience to emotional triggers can help you gain greater control over your emotional responses. This process is not about eliminating triggers but about learning how to engage with them in a way that encourages growth and self-awareness. With time and practice, you can shift these triggers from sources of stress to opportunities for personal development, deepening your understanding of yourself and improving your interactions with others.

Cultivating Self-Compassion and Kindness

Self-compassion involves treating yourself with the same kindness, care, and understanding that you would offer a dear friend. It is the gentle voice that reassures you, saying, "It's okay," when things go wrong. Self-compassion is essential for emotional health and well-being. It consists of three core components: self-kindness over harsh judgment, recognizing shared human experiences rather than feeling isolated, and mindfulness instead of becoming overly consumed by your thoughts. Unlike self-pity, which can trap you in a cycle of helplessness, self-compassion strengthens your ability to face difficulties with resilience. It is a reminder that mistakes are a natural part of life, not a reflection of your worth.

To cultivate self-compassion, engage in practices that encourage gentle self-acceptance. Loving-kindness meditation allows you to extend warmth and goodwill first to yourself and then to others. During this meditation, you silently repeat affirmations like "May I be happy" or "May I be at peace," helping to develop inner calm and acceptance. Another powerful exercise is writing a self-compassionate letter. When you feel discouraged or self-critical, write to yourself as if you were comforting a close friend. Offer understanding and encouragement, acknowledging that everyone struggles and that imperfection is part of being human. This practice can be profoundly healing, helping to reshape your internal dialogue into one that is more supportive and nurturing.

Kindness toward yourself and others creates an environment where growth can thrive. Engaging in small acts of self-care—such as resting when you are exhausted or forgiving yourself for minor mistakes—can significantly improve your mental and emotional well-being. Extending kindness in daily interactions, whether through a smile, a thoughtful word, or simply listening with empathy, strengthens your relationships and enriches your life. This outward expression of kindness reinforces your internal practice, creating a positive cycle that benefits both you and those around you. In this way, contributing kindness to the world also nurtures your personal development.

Self-criticism is one of the biggest obstacles to self-compassion. That nagging voice that insists "You're not good enough" or "You'll never succeed" can be relentless. Overcoming this requires a conscious effort to shift your perspective on negative self-talk. Begin by acknowledging the critical voice without judgment, then challenge its validity. Ask yourself if you would speak to a friend in the same way. By reframing these thoughts, you can begin to see imperfections as opportunities for growth rather than failures. Embracing your flaws allows you to learn from them, reinforcing a mindset that values progress over perfection. This shift in perspective is essential for developing a strong foundation of self-compassion.

As we explore self-compassion and kindness, we recognize their essential role in shaping emotional resilience. These practices help transform self-criticism into self-acceptance, fostering a more compassionate relationship with yourself. Developing inner kindness builds a strong framework for personal growth and healthier connections with others. This foundation paves the way for the next chapter, where we explore how trust and vulnerability can reshape relational patterns.

3

OVERCOMING BARRIERS TO INTIMACY

I magine standing on a bridge that stretches across a vast, flowing river. You are on one side, and everything you have ever wanted in a relationship is on the other. But the bridge wobbles with every step, and uncertainty grips you. This is what the fear of intimacy can feel like—an unsettling journey across an unsteady path, filled with the potential for connection yet shadowed by the fear of vulnerability.

Intimacy is more than just closeness; it is the deep trust and understanding that emerges when you allow someone to see your true self. It includes both emotional and physical aspects, forming the foundation of strong relationships. Emotional intimacy enables partners to share their deepest thoughts and feelings, creating a bond that withstands challenges over time. While often associated with emotional connection, physical intimacy provides the comfort of touch and warmth, reinforcing the human need for closeness. Together, these elements of intimacy strengthen trust, allowing relationships to grow in an atmosphere of safety and mutual respect.

. . .

The roots of intimacy fears often lie in past experiences and psychological influences. Childhood experiences can leave lasting imprints, shaping fears that carry into adulthood. Moments of rejection or dismissal when expressing vulnerability may lead to a lingering fear of abandonment, creating the belief that closeness comes with the risk of pain. This fear lingers, whispering that opening up may lead to loss. The brain's structure, particularly the amygdala and hippocampus, plays a key role in shaping these responses. These regions, influenced by past adverse experiences, can trigger heightened reactions when intimacy is at hand. It is not merely an emotional response but a physiological one, where the body remembers and reacts to patterns formed long ago. Understanding these origins helps explain why intimacy may feel more like a threat than a source of comfort.

Recognizing your fears around intimacy requires self-reflection and honesty. Begin by examining your past relationship patterns. What recurring themes do you notice? Were there times when you distanced yourself just as things became serious? Self-assessment tools can provide helpful insights, offering a structured way to explore these patterns. Through reflection, you may uncover a fear of rejection or a deeply held belief that vulnerability leads to pain. These realizations are not meant for self-judgment but for clarity. By identifying the fears that hold you back, you gain the ability to approach them with awareness and intention. This understanding is the first step in breaking down the barriers that stand between you and genuine connection.

Interactive Element: Intimacy Fear Self-Assessment

Take a moment to reflect on your fears surrounding intimacy. Ask yourself, "What triggers my fear of closeness?" and "How do these fears show up in my relationships?" Write down your thoughts, paying attention to patterns or recurring themes. This exercise can help you identify specific areas to address as you work toward overcoming these fears.

The impact of intimacy fears on relationships can be significant, often leading to a reluctance to form deep emotional connections. You might hesitate to share personal thoughts or feelings, even with those closest to you. This hesitation can create an emotional barrier, keeping others at a distance and preventing meaningful bonds from developing. Relationships may start to feel surface-level or unfulfilling, leaving you feeling alone even when surrounded by people. The fear convinces you that staying guarded is safer—that protecting yourself will prevent pain. However, this self-protection comes at a cost, keeping the deep connections you long for just out of reach. Recognizing these patterns is essential, as it allows you to face the fears that limit your ability to build strong, fulfilling relationships.

Strategies for Emotional Openness

Emotional openness can often feel out of reach, especially if you've spent years guarding your inner world. However, developing it isn't about plunging into the deep end without support; it's about learning to swim, one stroke at a time. Mindfulness exercises act as gentle waves that guide you toward greater emotional awareness. By practicing mindfulness, you train yourself to observe your emotions without judgment. Imagine sitting quietly, focusing on your breath, and allowing thoughts to pass like clouds. This practice helps you become more in tune with your feelings, making it easier to recognize them as they arise. With this awareness, you gain clarity, allowing you to express your emotions more authentically in relationships. This clarity is crucial for genuine connection, as it enables you to share your true self without fear of being misunderstood.

Overcoming emotional barriers requires a willingness to confront the fear of vulnerability. It's about embracing a mindset where challenges become opportunities for growth rather than obstacles. Start by recognizing that vulnerability is not a weakness but a sign of courage and strength. By accepting this, you create space for personal development, allowing yourself to step outside your comfort zone. Engaging in activities like journaling or creative expression can help expand your emotional range. These practices encourage you to explore your feelings in a safe space, gradually building confidence. Over time, you can dismantle the walls that have kept you closed off, making way for deeper, more authentic relationships.

Practicing emotional honesty is essential for building trust and intimacy. It involves being truthful about your feelings, even when discomfort arises. Communication exercises for couples can be particularly valuable here. Set aside time for active listening, where each partner takes turns speaking and listening without interruption. This practice not only enhances understanding but also reinforces respect and empathy. Role-playing scenarios for emotional honesty can also be beneficial, allowing you to rehearse difficult conversations in a non-threatening setting, which helps reduce anxiety and build confidence. As you commit to emotional honesty, you'll find your relationships becoming richer and more fulfilling, as both partners feel genuinely seen and heard.

The benefits of emotional openness extend beyond immediate relationships. They create a ripple effect, strengthening emotional bonds while fostering deeper trust and understanding. When you share your authentic self with another, you build a foundation of honesty that reinforces the relationship. This authenticity nurtures a sense of security, where both partners feel valued and accepted for who they truly are.

Emotional openness can be just as transformative in a professional setting. When leaders and team members communicate openly and sincerely, they cultivate an environment of trust and collaboration. Acknowledging vulnerabilities or admitting mistakes fosters stronger professional relationships, making colleagues feel more connected and understood. This openness encourages teamwork, sparks innovative problem-solving, and enhances workplace morale.

As trust deepens—whether in personal or professional settings—so does emotional connection, creating a positive cycle that strengthens relationships. The understanding that comes from this openness leads to more effective communication and conflict resolution, as all parties become more attuned to each other's needs and perspectives. This mutual understanding is the foundation of lasting, meaningful relationships—where love and respect thrive in personal life, and where mutual respect and synergy flourish in professional environments built on trust.

Building Trust in Relationships

Trust forms the foundation of any healthy relationship. It's that unspoken assurance that someone has your back—a bond that holds people together through both calm and stormy times. Trust isn't fixed; it evolves, built over time through consistent actions and words. Think of it as a reciprocal process, where both parties contribute to maintaining a balance of give and take. When nurtured, trust becomes resilient, capable of withstanding challenges. However, it is also fragile and can be easily damaged by dishonesty or betrayal. This duality requires attention and care, as the balance can shift in either direction, affecting the core of a relationship. Understanding the dynamics of trust means recognizing its fluid nature and the effort required to sustain it.

To build trust, consistent and reliable behavior is essential. It means keeping your word and speaking with sincerity. Reliability creates confidence, reinforcing the belief that you are dependable. Small acts —being on time, following through on commitments, or being present when needed—contribute significantly to trust. Open and honest communication is equally important. Transparency fosters clarity, reducing misunderstandings and creating a sense of security. Trust grows when both individuals feel they can speak freely without fear of judgment. Communication should be both verbal and non-verbal, as actions often carry more weight than words. Consistency in both speech and behavior establishes a strong foundation for trust.

Repairing broken trust requires dedication and sincerity. The first step is accountability—acknowledging the breach and taking full responsibility. This admission is crucial because it demonstrates a willingness to make amends. A sincere apology should follow, one that recognizes the hurt caused and expresses genuine remorse. An apology must be heartfelt, not merely obligatory, as a superficial one can deepen the divide. Rebuilding trust involves sustained, intentional actions over time. It's about proving, not just promising, that change is real. This may include setting new boundaries or consciously avoiding past mistakes. Patience is key, as trust takes time to restore. Each action serves as a building block, gradually reinforcing the relationship's integrity.

Trust-building exercises can be valuable tools for couples looking to strengthen or restore their connection. Engaging in activities that require cooperation and mutual reliance can be beneficial. Simple tasks, like cooking a meal together, where each person plays a role, reinforce the idea that you can depend on each other. Setting and working toward shared goals—such as saving for a vacation or planning a family event—also strengthens trust. This collaboration fosters deeper connection, as working towards a common goal requires communication, compromise, and trust. Such exercises build confidence in the partnership and help create a more harmonious relationship.

Trust Exercise: Strengthening Trust in Personal and Professional Relationships

In personal relationships, trust-building exercises—like the classic trust fall—can be a symbolic way to practice reliance on one another. Stand behind your partner as they fall backward, gently catching them. This simple yet meaningful activity encourages trust, vulnerability, and support. Afterward, discuss how it felt to depend on each other and explore ways to apply that trust to different aspects of your relationship.

Trust-building exercises can take a different but equally meaningful form in the workplace. One effective method is a feedback exchange exercise during a team meeting. Pair up with a colleague and share one thing you appreciate about each other's work and one area where you see room for growth. Frame this feedback constructively, focusing on collaboration and improvement. Discuss how you can support each other in developing your skills and succeeding in your roles.

Building trust at home or in the workplace requires continuous effort, reinforced by commitment, care, and respect. Strong relationships are built on consistent actions, open communication, and a willingness to acknowledge past mistakes. In professional settings, trust encourages transparency, teamwork, and mutual understanding. Each interaction—whether personal or professional—provides an opportunity to deepen trust and strengthen connections, fostering a positive and supportive environment.

The Role of Vulnerability in Connection

Many perceive vulnerability as a weakness, but in reality, it is one of the greatest strengths in a relationship. Think of it as the courage to lower your guard and let others see the real you—flaws and all. Embracing vulnerability means understanding that revealing your true self is not about exposing weaknesses but about fostering genuine connections. Sharing personal stories and raw truths invites others into your world. It's about saying, "This is me," and finding reassurance in knowing that authentic connection follows. This openness forms the foundation of trust and intimacy, allowing relationships to flourish in an environment of honesty and mutual respect. When you let your guard down, you give others permission to do the same, creating a bond built on shared understanding and empathy.

However, several barriers can make embracing vulnerability feel overwhelming. Fear of judgment whispers that revealing your inner thoughts and emotions might lead to rejection or ridicule. Cultural and societal norms often reinforce this fear, associating vulnerability with weakness. Many of us have learned to wear a brave face, suppress emotions, and avoid appearing too open. These ingrained beliefs create walls that separate us from true connection. Overcoming these barriers requires a shift in mindset—recognizing that vulnerability is not a risk but a bridge to deeper relationships. Acknowledging that everyone experiences these fears can cultivate a sense of solidarity, encouraging you to take the leap of faith required to be genuinely open.

To become more comfortable with vulnerability, consider engaging in practices that nurture emotional openness. Writing vulnerability letters can be a powerful exercise. Draft a letter to yourself or someone you trust, expressing thoughts and emotions you usually suppress. This practice helps articulate feelings and confront fears in a safe space. If you choose to share these letters, they can deepen understanding and trust. Participating in group discussions on personal topics can also be enlightening. In a supportive setting, discussing subjects that challenge your comfort zone allows you to hear others' experiences and share your own. These conversations break down isolation, reminding you that vulnerability is a shared human experience. Such exercises build confidence and highlight the beauty of genuine connection, where every story is valued and respected.

The impact of vulnerability on relationships is transformative. Consider a real-life example of a couple who, after years of emotional distance, broke the cycle by sharing their deepest fears and dreams. As they opened up, something shifted—the walls they had built began to crumble. Vulnerability became the force that held them together, strengthening a connection that once felt unreachable. Mutual openness is essential in partnerships. When both partners commit to honesty and emotional transparency, they create a cycle of trust and empathy. They become allies in their vulnerability, supporting each other through life's uncertainties and joys. This shared experience not only strengthens their bond but also enriches their lives, forming a partnership that is both resilient and deeply fulfilling.

Embracing Emotional Safety

Creating environments where emotional safety is prioritized is like building a sanctuary for the soul. It begins with setting and respecting boundaries, which serve as invisible lines that protect emotional well-being. Boundaries are not barriers; they are guide-lines that define what is acceptable and what is not. They create clarity in interactions, ensuring that each person feels secure and respected. Establishing these boundaries requires open communica-tion—expressing your needs while also listening to others without judgment. This process strengthens mutual respect and understand-ing, laying the foundation for a secure emotional space. Additionally, active listening and validation techniques further enhance this safety. When you actively listen, you fully engage with the speaker's emotions and thoughts, affirming their experience without imposing your own perspectives. Validation, on the other hand, acknowledges someone's feelings and experiences, reassuring them that they are heard and understood. Together, these practices cultivate an environ-ment where emotional safety can grow.

Emotional safety is vital for developing intimacy, as it provides the foundation upon which vulnerability can thrive. Without a sense of safety, sharing your deepest thoughts and emotions feels too risky—like entrusting your heart to someone without knowing if they will handle it with care. However, when emotional safety is present, it creates confidence in sharing emotions. You feel secure knowing your partner will respond with empathy and understanding rather than judgment or dismissal. This assurance encourages openness, allowing intimacy to deepen and flourish. In a secure emotional space, partners can explore their feelings and experiences together, strengthening their bond to withstand life's challenges. Emotional safety is not just a prerequisite for vulnerability; it is the core of any trusting relationship.

Establishing clear communication norms is essential for maintaining emotional safety, as they provide respectful and constructive interaction guidelines. Encouraging open discussions about needs and expectations creates a space where each person feels comfortable expressing themselves. Open communication allows for the negotiation of boundaries and the resolution of misunderstandings. By discussing expectations proactively, you not only prevent potential conflicts but also strengthen the relationship through shared understanding. Regular check-ins further enhance emotional safety, offering opportunities to address concerns or make adjustments that help sustain a supportive environment. These practices are not just about avoiding conflict but about fostering a culture of respect and empathy that influences every interaction.

Recognizing and addressing breaches of emotional safety is crucial to maintaining a healthy relationship. Breaches occur when someone crosses boundaries or communicates in a hurtful or dismissive way. It's important to identify these moments early and handle them constructively. Conflict resolution strategies play a key role in this process, emphasizing understanding and resolution rather than blame. These strategies prioritize listening to each other's perspectives and finding common ground. By focusing on the issue rather than the person, conflicts can be resolved in ways that strengthen the relationship instead of undermining it. Rebuilding trust and restoring emotional safety after a breach requires sincere apologies and a commitment to meaningful change. This process takes patience and consistent effort, as trust is regained through actions that demonstrate reliability and care over time.

As you cultivate emotional safety in your relationships, you create the conditions for deeper connections and greater intimacy. This secure foundation not only strengthens the relationship but also enhances your emotional well-being. When emotional safety is a priority, you can approach each interaction with confidence and openness, knowing that your emotions are respected and valued. This chapter has explored the significance of emotional safety, its impact, and practical ways to establish it in relationships. As we move forward, reflect on how these principles can transform your interactions, leading to more meaningful and fulfilling connections.

4

PRACTICAL STRATEGIES FOR CHANGE

T he scene unfolds in a cozy living room, where two people sit together, fully engaged in an intimate and meaningful conversation. It's not just a casual chat—it's an emotional check-in, a ritual they have established to deepen their connection. As they share their thoughts and feelings without judgment, a profound sense of closeness begins to take shape. This level of emotional intimacy strengthens relationships, creating a space where both individuals feel seen and valued. Emotional check-ins serve as powerful tools for building trust, inviting vulnerability, and fostering an environment where partners can openly explore their emotions. Setting aside regular time for these conversations prioritizes emotional connection, reinforcing the foundation of a strong and enduring bond.

Shared vulnerability exercises further enhance this closeness by encouraging partners to reveal their inner worlds. These exercises involve sharing personal stories, fears, and dreams—allowing each person to express their authentic self. Such openness deepens understanding and acceptance, as both partners learn to hold space for each other's experiences. Through shared vulnerability, you discover common ground, realizing that your fears and hopes are not so different after all. This mutual revelation can be both liberating and grounding, providing a foundation upon which trust and intimacy can grow.

Active listening techniques play a crucial role in strengthening this connection by enhancing your ability to understand and empathize with your partner. Reflective listening, where you paraphrase and repeat what your partner has said, demonstrates genuine engagement in the conversation. This approach not only clarifies communication but also validates your partner's feelings, reinforcing their importance. Paraphrasing exercises can be particularly effective, helping you distill the essence of your partner's message and ensuring mutual understanding. These techniques transform conversations into moments of connection, where both individuals feel heard, valued, and supported.

Expanding your emotional vocabulary is another essential step in deepening emotional intimacy. The ability to clearly articulate feelings enhances self-expression and strengthens communication. One valuable tool in this process is the emotion wheel, which helps identify and articulate subtle emotional nuances beyond basic descriptors like "happy" or "sad." Using this tool fosters a deeper awareness of your emotional experiences and provides a language for expressing them. Daily emotion journaling further supports this growth by offering a space to explore and record your feelings. Over time, these practices build a strong emotional vocabulary, equipping you to communicate with greater clarity, authenticity, and empathy.

Creating rituals for connection ensures that emotional intimacy remains a priority, embedding these practices into the core of your relationship. Weekly relationship meetings provide a structured opportunity to reflect on your relationship, address concerns, and celebrate progress. These meetings establish a dedicated time for connection, reinforcing the importance of nurturing your bond. Another powerful ritual is evening gratitude sharing, where partners take a moment to express appreciation for one another. This simple yet impactful practice cultivates positivity and reinforces the strengths of your relationship, deepening your commitment to each other.

Interactive Element: Emotional Vocabulary Exercise

Create an emotion wheel with your partner, with each section representing a different emotion, from joy to frustration. As you discuss your feelings, point to the section that best describes your emotional state. Use this as a guide to express your emotions more clearly, deepening understanding and connection.

By integrating these exercises and techniques into your relationship, you create a strong foundation for emotional connection. These strategies are not just tools but meaningful steps toward deeper understanding and intimacy, providing a framework for building a resilient and fulfilling relationship.

Step-by-Step Guides to Trust-Building

Building trust is a delicate balance that requires consistency and reliability. Imagine trust as the steady hand that guides you across a tightrope, ensuring each step feels secure. It begins with trust-building commitments—clear promises that lay the foundation for a strong, dependable relationship. These commitments might be as simple as following through on your word or as profound as sharing your honest thoughts, even when it's difficult. Setting and meeting expectations is another key component of this process. Expectations act as the roadmap for your relationship, outlining what each partner needs to feel valued and secure. By clearly communicating and consistently honoring these needs, you create a stable and supportive foundation.

Practical activities can further strengthen this foundation, turning the abstract concept of trust into tangible experiences. Consider joint problem-solving tasks where partners work together to overcome challenges—whether planning a trip, managing finances, or tackling a household project. These tasks require teamwork and open communication, reinforcing that you can rely on each other. Trust-building games can also be valuable. Simple activities like "Two Truths and a Lie" or team-based challenges borrowed from corporate settings encourage mutual understanding and strengthen connection. These exercises do more than entertain; they reveal deeper truths about each other in a safe and supportive environment, gradually strengthening trust through shared experiences.

Addressing trust issues requires patience and a thoughtful approach, as they are often tied to past betrayals or misunderstandings. Trust issue mapping is a useful tool in this process. By identifying previous breaches of trust and their impact, you can uncover patterns that contribute to lingering doubts. This process involves honest reflection and open dialogue, where both partners feel safe expressing their feelings without fear of criticism. Constructive feedback sessions provide another avenue for healing. These discussions should focus on expressing emotions and needs in a non-confrontational way, using "I" statements to take ownership of feelings and avoid blame. The goal is not to reopen old wounds but to rebuild trust through understanding, patience, and empathy.

Reinforcing trust over time is an ongoing commitment that requires regular attention and care. Trust check-ins provide an opportunity to assess the health of your relationship, addressing concerns before they become larger issues. These check-ins can be as simple as a weekly conversation over coffee, where both partners share their thoughts and feelings about the relationship. They serve as a reminder that trust is a living element of your connection, requiring nourishment and effort to thrive. Celebrating trust milestones is another meaningful way to reinforce trust. Whether it's an anniversary, a shared accomplishment, or a moment of growth, acknowledging these milestones strengthens your bond. It reinforces the understanding that trust is not just a destination but a continuous journey built on love, commitment, and mutual respect.

Overcoming the Withdrawal Reflex

The withdrawal reflex is a protective response, often shaped by early life experiences, where you instinctively pull away from emotional situations. Imagine a turtle retreating into its shell at the first sign of danger. This reflex can manifest in relationships as an automatic retreat when emotions run high, leaving your partner feeling shut out. Recognizing these patterns requires paying attention to when and how you withdraw. Do you pull back during conflicts or when vulnerability is needed? Identifying these moments helps you understand what triggers this response. Emotional triggers may include criticism, high-stress situations, or moments that require deep emotional engagement. These reactions are often rooted in past experiences that taught you to associate closeness with risk. By becoming aware of these patterns, you begin to see the withdrawal reflex not as a failure but as a learned behavior that can be reshaped.

Grounding exercises offer a practical way to counteract the tendency to withdraw. These techniques help you stay present in the moment, reducing the urge to retreat. Picture yourself in a moment of rising tension; instead of pulling away, focus on the sensation of your feet against the floor or the rhythm of your breathing. These simple acts anchor you, providing stability amidst emotional turmoil. Mindful pauses also play a crucial role. Before reacting—especially in heated moments—pause, take a deep breath, and allow your emotions to settle. This brief moment of reflection creates a buffer between the trigger and your response, giving you the space to choose a more thoughtful reaction. Developing these habits takes practice, but over time, they can gradually replace the instinct to withdraw with a more intentional approach.

Becoming comfortable with discomfort is another key step in overcoming withdrawal. Emotional discomfort isn't inherently negative; it signals growth and transformation. Think of it as strengthening a muscle—the initial strain is uncomfortable, but it leads to resilience. Facing emotional discomfort means deliberately engaging with situations that challenge your usual patterns. This might involve leaning into difficult conversations or allowing yourself to sit with uncomfortable emotions rather than avoiding them. Practicing emotional resilience in these moments builds tolerance, helping you endure and even embrace discomfort. Over time, you learn that discomfort is not a threat but an opportunity for deeper connection and self-awareness. Shifting your perspective in this way transforms fear into curiosity, reducing the instinct to retreat.

Accountability partners can provide meaningful support as you work to overcome withdrawal habits. These trusted individuals—whether friends, family members, or professional therapists—offer encouragement and perspective. Partnering for emotional support gives you someone to turn to when you feel the urge to retreat. They can provide a listening ear, a steady presence, or a gentle reminder to stay engaged. Maintaining open dialogue with an accountability partner is essential. Regularly discussing your progress, challenges, and victories keeps you accountable and provides valuable insights. This relationship reinforces that you are not alone in this journey and that support is always within reach. Through these partnerships, you develop a sense of shared purpose, strengthening your connections and counteracting the isolation that often accompanies withdrawal.

Conflict Resolution for Avoidant Personalities

Handling conflicts can feel overwhelming for anyone, but for those with avoidant tendencies, it often seems like navigating a labyrinth. Understanding your conflict style is the first step toward effective resolution. Some naturally gravitate toward avoidance, preferring to sidestep disputes entirely, while others take a more confrontational approach. Recognizing your style requires observing how you typically respond when disagreements arise. Do you find yourself withdrawing, hoping the issue will fade on its own? Or do you engage reluctantly, only to retreat at the first sign of tension? These patterns reveal much about your inherent approach to conflict. Differences in conflict styles also play a significant role in how misunderstandings develop. While some thrive on debate and direct communication, others prioritize harmony, sometimes at the expense of addressing important issues. This dynamic can lead to misinterpretation, where silence is mistaken for agreement or indifference rather than a coping mechanism. By identifying your conflict style and understanding these differences, you create a foundation for more effective engagement.

Effective communication during conflicts is essential for resolution, yet it can be challenging when emotions run high. One powerful strategy is using "I" statements, which express your feelings and needs without assigning blame. Instead of saying, "You never listen to me," try, "I feel unheard when I'm interrupted." This subtle shift changes the tone of the conversation, reducing defensiveness and encouraging understanding. Active listening is another key element. During disagreements, it's easy to focus on formulating your next response rather than truly hearing the other person. By concentrating on what your partner is saying and reflecting it back, you demonstrate empathy and validate their perspective. This approach clarifies communication and creates a sense of safety and respect, making room for productive dialogue. When both individuals feel heard and understood, conflict becomes less of a barrier and more of an opportunity to strengthen the connection.

Developing conflict resolution skills involves learning structured techniques to navigate disagreements constructively. Problem-solving frameworks provide a step-by-step approach, guiding you through identifying the issue, brainstorming solutions, and agreeing on a course of action. This method encourages collaboration and creativity, allowing both partners to contribute to a resolution. Compromise and negotiation techniques are equally important. These skills involve finding common ground and making thoughtful concessions so that both parties feel their needs are acknowledged. The goal is to create a solution that benefits everyone involved. By shifting the focus from individual grievances to shared goals, you turn conflict into an opportunity for growth and deeper understanding. While mastering these skills takes time and practice, they foster more harmonious relationships and a stronger sense of teamwork.

Creating a conflict-resolution plan provides a roadmap for managing disagreements before they escalate. A well-structured plan outlines specific steps to follow when conflicts arise, offering stability and predictability. It might include setting aside time to discuss issues calmly, away from distractions and heightened emotions. Personalized conflict action plans consider your unique dynamics and needs. They may involve identifying topics that should be off-limits during heated discussions or agreeing to take breaks when emotions become overwhelming. Setting conflict boundaries ensures that discussions remain respectful and productive, preventing them from spiraling into unhelpful arguments. These boundaries act as guardrails, keeping the focus on the issue at hand and protecting the relationship from unnecessary harm. By proactively identifying potential challenges and agreeing on how to navigate them, you create a framework that supports constructive resolution and strengthens your partnership.

Balancing Independence and Interdependence

Navigating relationships requires understanding the delicate balance between independence and interdependence. Independence is about maintaining your identity, pursuing personal goals, and nurturing self-reliance. It's the freedom to express yourself without losing your sense of self within a relationship. However, independence should not be mistaken for isolation. It is entirely possible to be independent while remaining deeply connected to others.

Interdependence, on the other hand, is built on mutual support and collaboration. It acknowledges that you and your partner are stronger together while still maintaining individuality. This balance creates a relationship where both partners feel valued and supported, reinforcing trust and emotional security.

Cultivating healthy independence starts with setting personal goals. Define clear objectives for yourself—whether in career aspirations, hobbies, or self-development. Pursuing individual goals strengthens your identity and ensures that your sense of self remains intact within the relationship. Prioritizing self-care is equally important. Engage in activities that rejuvenate and center you, such as exercising, reading, or spending time in nature. These routines are not just about relaxation; they reinforce personal well-being, allowing you to bring your best self into the relationship.

Strengthening interdependence requires an intentional approach. Collaborative decision-making is essential, ensuring that both partners have a voice in choices that affect them. Open discussions and mutual respect foster a sense of unity and shared purpose. Shared responsibilities and goals further reinforce interdependence. Whether managing household tasks or planning for the future, working together builds trust and deepens the connection. This dynamic enhances communication and promotes a greater understanding of each other's strengths and needs, forming a strong foundation for mutual support.

Balancing independence and interdependence can be challenging but ultimately rewarding. Regular self-check-ins are essential. Take time to assess your relationship dynamics—do you feel too enmeshed or too distant? These reflections help identify areas that may need adjustment, allowing you to make conscious choices about how you engage with each other. Adjusting relationship dynamics might involve setting new boundaries or renegotiating roles and expectations. These shifts ensure that both partners feel comfortable and fulfilled, creating a relationship that honors individuality while embracing togetherness. Since relationships evolve, this balance requires ongoing attention and effort.

Ultimately, finding harmony between independence and interdependence strengthens your relationship, creating a partnership where both individuals can grow and thrive. As you reflect on these principles, consider how they can enhance your interactions, shaping a relationship that is both supportive and empowering. Balancing these elements lays the groundwork for a fulfilling connection, preparing you for the next steps in your personal and relational growth journey. In the next chapter, we will explore how these foundational elements contribute to deeper emotional intimacy and long-term relationship resilience.

5

EMPLOYMENT AND PERSONAL LIFE BALANCE

P icture this: a bustling office, fluorescent lights buzzing overhead, and the steady hum of conversation filling the air. You sit at your desk, methodically working through your tasks—a solitary figure amid a sea of colleagues. While others gather in animated clusters, discussing projects and brainstorming ideas, you find solace in the quiet focus of your work. This scene is familiar to many who experience avoidant attachment in the workplace, where professional environments can feel as daunting as personal relationships. The demands of teamwork, networking, and collaboration often conflict with an inherent preference for independence, creating a complex dynamic that impacts career growth and personal satisfaction.

Recognizing avoidant behaviors in the workplace is the first step toward understanding their effect on your professional life. These behaviors often manifest subtly, shaping interactions and influencing career progression. A common indicator is avoidance of team projects. Sharing responsibilities or relying on others can trigger discomfort, leading to a reluctance to participate in collaborative efforts. This hesitancy stems from a fear of vulnerability and a preference for self-reliance, where the unpredictability of teamwork feels overwhelming. While working independently may provide a sense of control, it can also limit exposure to diverse perspectives and hinder opportunities for innovation.

Reluctance to engage in networking is another hallmark of avoidant attachment in professional settings. Networking events—where small talk and introductions serve as currency—can feel overwhelming and inauthentic. The pressure to present a polished version of yourself may lead to withdrawal as you struggle to balance authenticity with professional expectations. This hesitation often results in missed opportunities to build valuable connections that could support career advancement. While networking is a key aspect of professional development, offering pathways to mentorship and collaboration, the discomfort it brings can keep you on the periphery, observing rather than participating in the conversations that drive growth.

Avoidant attachment can also have a profound impact on career development, influencing professional relationships and limiting growth opportunities. One major challenge is the reluctance to pursue leadership roles. Leadership requires navigating complex interpersonal dynamics and managing diverse teams—tasks that can feel daunting for those who tend to avoid vulnerability. Fear of exposure and self-doubt can lead to hesitation in stepping into leadership positions, reinforcing a cycle of isolation and stagnation. This reluctance prevents the development of essential leadership skills and can stall career progression. However, embracing leadership opportunities, even in small steps, can help break this pattern and build confidence in managing relationships and responsibilities.

Missed opportunities for collaboration are another consequence of avoidant attachment in the workplace. Collaboration fuels innovation, allowing ideas to evolve through collective input. However, discomfort with sharing thoughts and trusting others with ideas can create barriers to teamwork. The fear of judgment or rejection may lead to working in silos, relying solely on individual effort rather than engaging in co-creation. While this approach offers control and autonomy, it limits the potential for creativity and problem-solving that emerges from diverse perspectives. Seeking mentorship and gradually stepping into collaborative spaces can help overcome these barriers, opening doors to new opportunities for professional growth and meaningful connections.

Adapting requires a conscious effort to engage in collaboration while maintaining your sense of independence. Participating in team-building exercises can provide a structured way to connect with colleagues. These activities create a safe space to explore teamwork dynamics, emphasizing trust and rapport. By stepping outside your comfort zone in these settings, you can gradually acclimate to collaborative environments, learning to balance autonomy with the benefits of teamwork. These exercises not only strengthen your interpersonal skills but also cultivate a sense of connection, helping you feel more engaged with your colleagues.

Seeking mentorship is another effective strategy for adapting to team dynamics. Mentors offer valuable insights into professional environments, providing support and guidance as you explore new opportunities. They can help identify areas for growth, offering a perspective that bridges your independent work style with the collaborative aspects of your role. Mentors also serve as role models, demonstrating how to navigate workplace challenges with confidence and composure. By building a mentorship relationship, you gain access to a wealth of knowledge and experience, empowering you to step into roles that align with your professional aspirations.

Leveraging strengths in professional roles is essential for those with avoidant tendencies, as it allows you to excel while staying true to your natural preferences. Independence and self-reliance are often strengths that come naturally, enabling you to manage tasks efficiently with minimal supervision. In roles that require focus and attention to detail, your ability to work autonomously becomes an asset, allowing you to thrive in environments that value individual contributions. By highlighting these strengths, you can carve out a role where your skills are recognized and utilized effectively.

Analytical and problem-solving skills are additional strengths that individuals with avoidant attachment often possess. These abilities allow you to approach challenges with a logical and methodical mindset, breaking down complex problems into manageable steps. Your capacity to analyze data and develop solutions is especially valuable in roles requiring strategic thinking and innovation. By using these skills effectively, you can make meaningful contributions to projects, strengthening your professional reputation and advancing your career.

Interactive Element: Professional Strengths Inventory

Take a moment to reflect on your professional strengths. Consider the qualities and skills that set you apart in the workplace. Create a list of these strengths, focusing on both technical and interpersonal attributes. Use this inventory to identify roles and opportunities that align with your abilities. Doing so will help you approach your career with confidence and clarity.

As you work through the challenges of avoidant attachment in professional settings, remember that your journey is personal and evolving. By recognizing your behavioral patterns and their impact, you can make conscious adjustments, allowing yourself to thrive in team environments. Leveraging your strengths will not only help you adapt but also empower you to build a fulfilling and successful career.

Trusting Others in Professional Settings

In the fast-paced world of work, trust is a cornerstone of professional success. This unseen force transforms teams into cohesive units and elevates ordinary tasks into extraordinary achievements. Trust-based collaboration is essential—it is the glue that allows diverse talents to come together, creating a sense of unity and shared purpose. When trust thrives, so does creativity. Employees feel empowered to contribute ideas without fear of judgment, leading to innovative solutions and meaningful progress.

In contrast, a lack of trust can stifle communication, creating barriers that hinder growth and collaboration. Trust is also essential for effective delegation, a critical element in any thriving workplace. Delegation is more than just assigning tasks; it is about entrusting responsibilities to others with confidence in their abilities. This trust enhances productivity and empowers employees, reinforcing a sense of ownership and accountability that drives projects forward. When leaders delegate with trust, they demonstrate belief in their team's capabilities, inspiring confidence and dedication.

Building trust with colleagues requires a commitment to transparent communication. Open dialogue lays the foundation for honesty, ensuring that expectations and intentions are clear. This transparency reduces misunderstandings and aligns team members toward common goals. It involves sharing both successes and challenges, creating an environment where everyone feels informed and engaged. Consistency in fulfilling commitments further strengthens trust. When you consistently follow through on promises, you establish a reputation for reliability. This reassures colleagues that they can depend on you, deepening professional connections. Trust is about aligning words with actions and demonstrating integrity in every task. Over time, these practices cultivate mutual respect and dependability, both essential for a thriving workplace.

Yet, barriers to trust often emerge, shaped by skepticism and past experiences. Managing doubts about colleagues requires an open-minded approach, recognizing that trust is built through shared experiences over time. Developing a trust-building mindset is key. This mindset embraces vulnerability and openness, understanding that trust requires a willingness to take risks. It means actively choosing to trust, even when uncertainties linger. By focusing on positive interactions and shared achievements, you can gradually overcome skepticism and nurture stronger connections. This trans-formation takes patience and empathy, acknowledging that everyone brings their own history and hesitations into the workplace.

Feedback plays a pivotal role in building trust. Constructive feedback serves as a tool for growth, offering insights that enhance both performance and relationships. Seeking feedback demonstrates a willingness to learn and improve, signaling respect for others' perspectives. Effective feedback requires tact and sensitivity, focusing on behaviors rather than personal attributes. This approach culti-vates a culture of continuous improvement, where feedback is seen as a valuable resource rather than criticism. Implementing feedback involves more than just acknowledging it—it requires taking action-able steps for improvement. Integrating feedback into your work shows commitment to personal and professional growth, reinforcing trust with colleagues. Establishing cooperative work relationships depends on this cycle of feedback and trust. When team members feel valued and heard, they are more likely to engage and contribute, creating a dynamic and supportive work environment.

In professional settings, trust is not just an individual responsibility but a collective one. It requires each team member to engage with openness, honesty, and a willingness to support one another. By prioritizing trust in your interactions, you lay the foundation for a workplace where collaboration and innovation thrive. Trust is the bridge that connects ideas, people, and opportunities, turning everyday tasks into meaningful achievements. In this interconnected professional space, the ability to trust and be trusted is a powerful asset that fuels success and fulfillment.

As you move through these dynamics, remember that trust is not a fixed destination but an evolving process shaped by each interaction and experience. Embrace this journey with curiosity and compassion, knowing that every step forward brings you closer to a workplace where trust and collaboration become second nature. The next chapter will explore how personal growth and professional development intersect, guiding you toward a more balanced and fulfilling life.

Make a Difference with Your Review

Unlock the Power of Connection

"The meaning of life is to find your gift. The purpose of life is to give it away." — Pablo Picasso.

When we give without expecting anything in return, we open doors to happiness—not just for others but also for ourselves. Let's work together to make a difference!

Would you help someone like you—someone curious about avoidant attachment but unsure where to begin?

My goal with *Avoidant Attachment Recovery Solution* is to make healing and connection accessible and achievable for everyone. But to reach more people who need this message, I need your help.

Most people rely on reviews when choosing their next book. That's where you come in. By leaving a review, you could inspire someone to take their first step toward inner confidence and healthier relationships.

Your review matters.

- A person breaks free from emotional barriers.
- A reader learns how to overcome their fear of intimacy.
- An individual reclaims their inner confidence.
- A person transforms their life and builds lasting, secure relationships.

It takes less than a minute, costs nothing, and could change someone's life.

To leave a review, scan the QR code below or visit the link:

https://www.amazon.com/review/review-your-purchases/?asin=
B0F3W448ZW

If you enjoy helping others, you are my person. Thank you for supporting this mission and participating in this journey.

With gratitude,

Luzivette Martinez

6

CULTIVATING STRONGER EMOTIONAL BONDS

I n the heart of a bustling city, a couple finds solace in their shared morning ritual—brewing coffee together before the day begins. This small yet meaningful practice strengthens their connection beyond words, grounding them in each other's presence. Emotional bonding, built on shared experiences and mutual understanding, forms the foundation of lasting relationships. It's about being emotionally available and present, creating a space where both partners feel seen and valued. This connection deepens through shared moments, crafting cherished memories that serve as the foundation for a relationship strong enough to withstand life's challenges and celebrate its joys.

Regularly setting aside quality time is essential for strengthening these connections. For instance, designate a specific evening each week to disconnect from the digital world and focus entirely on each other. Whether it's a simple dinner at home, a walk in the park, or an activity you both enjoy, these moments go beyond physical presence —they encourage emotional engagement, allowing for deeper communication and understanding. Rituals of appreciation and gratitude also play a vital role. Taking time to acknowledge and express what you value about your partner—through a handwritten note, a thoughtful text, or a sincere compliment—reinforces your emotional bond. These small yet intentional acts serve as reminders of the love and respect you share.

Shared activities further strengthen emotional bonds by creating opportunities for collaboration and mutual enjoyment. Whether tackling a home improvement project or exploring a new hobby together, these experiences foster teamwork and creativity. They encourage you to rely on each other's strengths and support one another through challenges, reinforcing a sense of unity. Participating in community events also strengthens your connection as a couple. Whether volunteering for a local cause or attending a cultural festival, these shared experiences broaden your perspective and solidify your bond through common goals and values.

Encouraging vulnerability is key to deepening emotional bonds. Sharing personal stories and experiences, even the difficult ones, paves the way for greater intimacy. It's about allowing yourself to be truly seen, trusting that your partner will honor your vulnerability with care. This openness invites reciprocity, creating a cycle of mutual trust and empathy. Making space for open emotional expression further solidifies this bond. Regularly checking in with each other—discussing both the highs and lows—builds a foundation of honesty and transparency, essential for a resilient and lasting relationship.

Reflection Exercise: The Memory Jar

Create a memory jar together. Each time you share a meaningful experience or moment of joy, write it down on a small piece of paper and place it in the jar. Over time, watch as it fills with memories that reflect your journey. Read a few together on special occasions or whenever you need a reminder of your bond. This simple yet powerful exercise preserves your shared history and strengthens your emotional connection.

Understanding emotional bonding means recognizing the power of presence and shared experiences in nurturing lasting connections. By intentionally engaging in practices that encourage quality time, shared activities, and open vulnerability, you reinforce the emotional ties that bring you closer. These bonds, built on mutual respect and understanding, create a strong foundation for a relationship that can thrive through life's challenges.

Enhancing Communication with Loved Ones

Effective communication is the foundation that sustains connection in relationships. It involves expressing your thoughts clearly and directly to ensure your message is understood without ambiguity. Clarity means saying what you mean without room for misinterpretation. Directness involves cutting through distractions and speaking your truth with honesty and respect. Yet, words are just one part of the conversation. Non-verbal cues—like a reassuring touch, eye contact, or the tone of your voice—play a crucial role in conveying your message. These signals often speak louder than words, adding depth and emotion to your interactions. Being mindful of these nuances enriches conversations and strengthens understanding between you and your loved ones.

Different communication styles influence how we interact. Some people communicate passively, avoiding confrontation and expressing their needs indirectly. Others are assertive, speaking openly while respecting others. Some lean toward aggressive communication, dominating conversations and dismissing opposing views. Recognizing these styles is essential. It allows you to adjust your approach to suit the person you are engaging with. For instance, if someone is passive, create a safe space that encourages them to share their thoughts. If they are assertive, match their directness while maintaining respect. Understanding these preferences helps you adapt your style for more effective and meaningful interactions.

. . .

Communication barriers often stem from assumptions and misunderstandings. We may assume we know what someone means without fully listening or jump to conclusions based on past experiences. These barriers cloud interactions, leading to frustration and disconnection. To overcome them, start by questioning your assumptions. Are you interpreting their words accurately or filtering them through your biases? Managing emotional reactions can also be helpful. Take a deep breath before responding or pause to reflect. These small moments allow you to process emotions and respond thoughtfully rather than impulsively. Addressing these barriers directly leads to more authentic and productive conversations.

Establishing communication agreements can further improve understanding. These agreements are not rigid rules but practical guidelines that facilitate smoother interactions. Setting ground rules —such as listening without interrupting or addressing issues calmly —creates a respectful dialogue framework. Regular check-ins are also beneficial. Set aside time to reflect on how you communicate, what works, and what needs improvement. These check-ins provide a space to express concerns or frustrations before they escalate. Committing to these agreements nurtures an environment where open and honest communication can thrive, strengthening your relationships.

Interactive Element: Communication Style Quiz

Consider taking a communication style quiz with your loved ones and discussing the results openly. Explore how each person's style shapes interactions and use these insights to adjust your communication approach. Ensuring your style aligns with each person's needs and preferences fosters better understanding and strengthens your connection. This exercise helps highlight the unique dynamics within your relationships, creating a more meaningful and effective way to communicate.

Navigating Relationship Dynamics

Every relationship is a balance of dynamics, where power and roles shift over time. Understanding these shifts in your interactions is crucial. Imagine a seesaw where balance depends on both sides working in harmony. Power dynamics often tip this balance, influencing decisions and determining who feels heard. It's not always about dominance; sometimes, subtle cues dictate who leads the conversation and who follows. When balanced, both partners feel valued and respected. However, if one person consistently holds more power, it can lead to resentment and tension, surfacing as minor disagreements or deeper conflicts. Recognizing these dynamics and their impact on your relationship is the first step toward creating a more equal and fulfilling partnership.

Role expectations add another layer to relationship dynamics. These expectations often stem from societal norms, personal experiences, or observed family roles. You may expect your partner to manage finances while you handle household responsibilities, or vice versa. While roles can provide structure, they can also become limiting, stifling individuality and personal growth. It's important to assess whether these expectations support or restrict your relationship. If one partner feels confined to a role, it can create friction and dissatisfaction. By openly discussing and redefining roles, you ensure they align with both partners' needs and strengths, allowing each person to contribute in a way that feels authentic and fulfilling.

Adjusting to changing dynamics requires flexibility and a willingness to grow. Relationships are not static; they evolve as both partners change. Embracing this evolution means being open to redefining roles and responsibilities as needed. For instance, if one partner takes on a demanding job, the other might step up in different areas at home. This adaptability builds resilience, helping the relationship withstand external pressures and internal shifts. Change should not be seen as a threat but as an opportunity for growth and deeper connection. When both partners approach change with an open mind, they create a strong, responsive partnership that can thrive in any situation.

Conflicts often arise when dynamics shift, creating tension that strains the relationship. Identifying the source of stress is crucial for resolution. It could stem from poor communication about shifting roles or unmet expectations. Once identified, addressing these issues with constructive conflict resolution strategies can help. Setting aside time to discuss concerns ensures both partners feel heard. The key is to approach conflict with an attitude of understanding rather than blame. By focusing on the issue rather than assigning fault, you can resolve conflicts in a way that strengthens the relationship through shared understanding and compromise.

Growth is essential for strengthening relationship dynamics. Setting mutual goals encourages both partners to work toward a shared vision, whether it's financial planning, travel, or personal development. These goals create a sense of unity and purpose, reinforcing the relationship. Engaging in continuous learning together also strengthens the bond. It could involve taking a class, exploring new hobbies, or discussing books and ideas. These shared experiences expand perspectives and deepen connections, building a fulfilling and enduring relationship. As you grow individually and as a couple, you create a strong, adaptable dynamic that can withstand life's challenges and opportunities.

The Power of Empathetic Listening

Empathetic listening goes beyond simply hearing words—it's about truly understanding and connecting with another person's feelings and experiences. Unlike active listening, which focuses on attentively capturing the speaker's message, empathetic listening engages with the emotional depth behind the words. It requires stepping into the speaker's perspective, striving to experience their emotions as if they were your own. This practice strengthens connections, as empathy bridges the gap between individuals, allowing for genuine understanding. When you engage in empathetic listening, you are not just a passive recipient of information but an active participant in the emotional exchange, ensuring the speaker feels truly heard and valued.

Developing empathetic listening skills involves key practices that can transform your interactions. Reflective listening exercises are a good starting point. These involve paraphrasing or summarizing the speaker's words and reflecting them back. This ensures clarity while demonstrating your engagement and understanding. Practicing silence and patience is equally important. The urge to offer advice or solutions often overshadows the speaker's need to feel heard. Allowing moments of silence gives the speaker space to process their thoughts and emotions, encouraging a more thoughtful and meaningful dialogue. While this patience can be challenging, especially when you want to help, it reinforces the speaker's sense of being genuinely understood.

Awareness and effort can help overcome barriers that often hinder empathetic listening. Personal biases and judgments can cloud our ability to listen with empathy, leading to assumptions and misunderstandings. To manage these biases, approach each conversation with an open mind, setting aside preconceived notions. Techniques such as mindfulness or self-reflection can also help develop emotional openness. These practices encourage awareness of your own emotional responses, allowing you to engage in interactions with curiosity rather than judgment. By cultivating a mindset that values understanding over assumption, you create the foundation for deeper and more meaningful connections.

The impact of empathetic listening can be transformative, as seen in many real-life situations. Consider a couple struggling to connect due to differing communication styles. By consciously practicing empathetic listening, they began to truly understand each other's perspectives, leading to a profound shift in their relationship. Listening with empathy allowed them to appreciate each other's emotions and experiences, strengthening their connection and trust. Encouraging mutual empathy in interactions further amplifies this impact. When both individuals practice empathetic listening, it creates a cycle of understanding and support, ensuring that each person feels valued and heard. This shared empathy strengthens relationships, building a foundation of trust and respect that can withstand the challenges of everyday life.

Celebrating Diversity in Relationships

Diversity plays a vital role in shaping how we connect and understand one another in relationships. Recognizing diverse experiences means acknowledging the different ways people relate to each other, influenced by cultural backgrounds, personal histories, and unique family structures. Cultural diversity adds depth to relationships, offering perspectives shaped by traditions, values, and customs from around the world. Similarly, personal diversity—rooted in individual life experiences and personal growth—contributes to the uniqueness of each connection. Diverse family structures, from nuclear families to extended kinship networks, challenge traditional definitions of family, encouraging a more inclusive understanding of what family truly means.

Building inclusivity in relationships requires intention and a willingness to embrace differences. One effective approach is learning about and respecting cultural traditions. This might involve participating in cultural festivals or simply engaging in conversations about family customs. These actions show respect and a genuine interest in understanding others, creating a more inclusive environment. Encouraging open discussions about diversity also strengthens relationships. Providing space for conversations about cultural practices, religious beliefs, or personal values fosters trust and deeper connection. When diversity is openly acknowledged and discussed, partners can explore each other's perspectives, break down barriers, and build meaningful bridges of connection.

While diversity enhances relationships, it can also present challenges. Cultural misunderstandings often stem from assumptions or stereotypes. Addressing these requires patience and an open mind—seeing misunderstandings as opportunities to learn rather than obstacles. By actively seeking to understand different viewpoints, potential conflicts can become moments of connection. Viewing diversity as a strength means recognizing that differences enhance rather than detract. Varied perspectives bring creativity and new approaches to problem-solving, enriching relationships with fresh insights and adaptability.

Creating an inclusive environment means cultivating a space where diversity is not just accepted but valued and celebrated. Thoughtful communication plays a crucial role in this process. Choosing respectful language, avoiding marginalizing terms, and being mindful of cultural sensitivities all contribute to inclusivity. Acknowledging and celebrating diverse milestones—whether cultural holidays, personal achievements, or individual contributions—reinforces the importance of diversity. These celebrations highlight the value of differences, strengthening relationships with a sense of belonging and shared appreciation.

Diversity in relationships is not just about tolerating differences but actively engaging with them. By embracing diversity, we open ourselves to new experiences and perspectives that enrich our connections and our lives. This chapter has explored the impact of diversity and provided strategies for embracing it in relationships. As we move forward, let us carry these insights into our interactions, fostering an environment where diversity is honored and relationships thrive.

7

INTEGRATING MINDFULNESS AND RELAXATION

Walking through a crowded park, you might notice a person sitting quietly on a bench, eyes closed, seemingly unaffected by the noise around them. They appear at peace, wrapped in a sense of calm amidst the chaos. This serene presence often reflects the practice of mindfulness—a state of awareness that allows individuals to focus on the present moment with openness and curiosity. Mindfulness isn't about eliminating thoughts or emotions but about acknowledging them without judgment and letting them pass. This practice strengthens emotional clarity, offering insights into our mental state that might otherwise go unnoticed. For adults navigating personal and professional complexities, mindfulness provides a path to greater self-awareness and emotional resilience. By developing this practice, you can learn to respond to life's challenges with composure and clarity, improving your overall well-being.

At its core, mindfulness is the practice of maintaining moment-by-moment awareness of your thoughts, emotions, bodily sensations, and surroundings. It involves tuning into the present and embracing each experience without labeling it as good or bad. This awareness sharpens perception, helping you see situations with greater clarity.

The impact of mindfulness on emotional clarity is profound. By staying present, you become more attuned to your emotional states, recognizing patterns and triggers that shape your reactions. This awareness transforms how you interact with yourself and others, making it easier to manage emotions with confidence and understanding. Mindfulness is not a destination but an ongoing journey of self-discovery, deepening your connection with yourself and the world around you.

Practicing mindfulness offers significant benefits, particularly in emotional regulation. It encourages a balanced approach to emotions, allowing you to observe feelings without becoming overwhelmed by them. This detachment creates space for processing emotions in a constructive way, reducing the effects of stress and anxiety. Mindfulness helps you maintain inner peace, even in difficult situations. It enables you to respond to challenges with intention rather than reacting impulsively. This shift in perspective strengthens emotional resilience and enhances your ability to handle life's ups and downs. Additionally, mindfulness improves cognitive functions such as concentration and memory, supporting overall mental well-being. Incorporating mindfulness into your daily life builds a foundation for emotional stability and personal growth.

Several mindfulness practices can enhance emotional clarity and self-awareness, each offering a unique way to stay present. One effective practice is body scan meditation, which involves mentally scanning your body from head to toe, noticing any sensations or tension without judgment. This practice strengthens self-awareness by helping you connect with your physical state, highlighting areas that need care or attention. Another valuable practice is mindful observation of thoughts and emotions. This involves sitting quietly, allowing your thoughts and feelings to surface, and observing them without attachment. Over time, this practice helps you recognize emotional patterns and triggers, offering deeper insights into your mental state. By regularly engaging in these techniques, you can develop a greater understanding of yourself, improving emotional clarity and overall well-being.

Incorporating mindfulness into daily routines can help maintain emotional clarity. Mindful eating, for example, encourages you to fully engage with each bite, focusing on the flavors and textures of your food. This practice enhances your appreciation of meals and promotes a healthier relationship with food. Walking meditation is another simple yet effective technique. As you walk, pay attention to the sensation of your feet touching the ground and the rhythm of your breath. This practice keeps you anchored in the present moment, creating a sense of calm and awareness. By integrating these mindfulness habits into your daily life, you build a strong foundation of emotional awareness that supports overall well-being.

Despite its benefits, staying mindful can be challenging, especially with the constant distractions of modern life. It's common for thoughts to interrupt meditation, pulling your attention away from the present. To manage these distractions, acknowledge them without judgment and gently bring your focus back to your breath or chosen point of concentration. Developing patience and persistence is essential to strengthening mindfulness. Like any skill, it requires regular practice and commitment. Approaching it with curiosity and openness allows you to explore and grow at your own pace. Embracing these challenges deepens your mindfulness practice and enhances emotional clarity.

Interactive Element: Mindfulness Daily Log

Consider keeping a daily mindfulness journal to track your progress and reflections. Record the practices you engage in each day, along with any insights or challenges you experience. This journal can serve as a valuable tool for self-reflection and personal growth, reinforcing your commitment to mindfulness.

Relaxation Techniques to Reduce Stress

In the hustle and bustle of daily life, stress often feels like an unwelcome companion that refuses to leave your side. From looming deadlines to social obligations, something always demands your attention. This is where the art of relaxation becomes essential. Think of relaxation as your mind's reset button—a way to counterbalance the relentless pressure of stress. It creates a sanctuary where your body and mind can recover, allowing you to approach challenges with renewed energy and clarity. Physiologically, relaxation lowers heart rate and blood pressure, reduces muscle tension, and slows breathing, helping the body return to a calm state. Psychologically, it alleviates anxiety, improves mood, and enhances overall mental health. By making relaxation a regular part of your routine, you're not just taking a break—you're investing in your well-being.

Guided relaxation techniques can serve as powerful tools for managing stress. Progressive muscle relaxation, for example, involves systematically tensing and then relaxing each muscle group in your body. This method not only relieves physical tension but also increases awareness of stress's physical effects. Imagine lying in a quiet room, starting with your toes and working your way up to your head, feeling each muscle release its tension. Guided imagery is another effective technique. It involves visualizing a tranquil scene, such as a beach or a forest, and immersing yourself in its sensory details. These mental escapes create distance from stressors, even if only for a few minutes, allowing for greater mental clarity and peace.

Incorporating relaxation into your daily life doesn't require a complete overhaul of your schedule. Instead, it's about finding small moments to integrate these practices into your routine. Set aside a few minutes each evening to unwind, perhaps with herbal tea and soft music. This dedicated relaxation time signals to your body that it's time to shift gears. Creating a calming environment at home can also enhance relaxation. Try dimming the lights, using soothing scents like lavender or chamomile, and eliminating unnecessary distractions. These small adjustments can make a significant difference, transforming your home into a space where relaxation happens naturally.

Technology, often viewed as a source of stress, can also be a valuable ally in your relaxation journey. Apps like Calm and Headspace offer guided meditations and relaxation exercises that you can access anytime, anywhere. These platforms provide structured sessions ranging from a few minutes to longer practices, making it easy to customize relaxation to fit your needs. Online guided meditation sessions are another helpful resource, offering both structure and a sense of community as you explore different techniques. These sessions can be particularly beneficial if you prefer guided instruction or enjoy connecting with others who share a similar goal. By using technology wisely, you can make relaxation a consistent practice rather than an occasional indulgence.

Staying Present in the Moment

Amid the whirlwind of daily life, staying present can feel like an elusive goal. Yet, being present is not about changing reality—it's about fully inhabiting the moment you're in. When you focus on the present, you tune into the here and now, experiencing life as it unfolds. This awareness enriches your experiences, allowing you to appreciate the subtleties of everyday life. The benefits go beyond mindfulness; they positively impact your mental and emotional well-being. You gain clarity, reducing anxiety about the future and regrets about the past. By embracing the present, you cultivate a sense of peace and contentment, finding joy in life's simple moments.

You can enhance your presence throughout the day with specific techniques that anchor you in the moment. Focused breathing exercises are a simple yet powerful tool. Paying attention to your breath creates a focal point that shifts your awareness away from distractions. Try inhaling deeply through your nose, holding for a few seconds, and then exhaling slowly through your mouth. This rhythmic breathing calms the mind and centers your thoughts. Mindfulness reminders can also help. Set an alarm or use an app to prompt you to pause and take a few deep breaths throughout the day. These gentle cues serve as checkpoints, bringing you back to the present.

To deepen your connection with the present, fully engage in daily activities through mindful observation and participation. When listening to others, give them your full attention, setting aside internal distractions. This mindful listening strengthens under-standing and deepens connections. Similarly, immerse yourself in tasks and hobbies. Whether gardening, cooking, or painting, engage fully with the experience. Notice the textures, colors, and sounds, allowing yourself to be completely involved in the process. These moments of deep focus create a flow state, where time seems to slow, and you experience genuine fulfillment.

Distractions are inevitable, but they don't have to pull you away from the present. Managing them effectively helps you maintain focus even in chaotic environments. Start by identifying common distrac-tions—whether digital notifications, background noise, or wandering thoughts. Once you recognize them, refocus by taking a short break to reset or using grounding techniques to stay centered. Acknowl-edging distractions without judgment is also helpful. When they arise, observe them briefly and then gently bring your focus back to the task at hand. This practice builds resilience, teaching you how to handle interruptions with ease and stay present in any situation.

Emotional Regulation through Mindfulness

Picture a stormy sea—the waves crash with intensity, yet beneath the turbulent surface, the ocean remains calm and steady. This mirrors the role of mindfulness in regulating emotions, providing a stable foundation even when life's challenges feel overwhelming. Mindful-ness helps maintain emotional balance by increasing awareness, allowing you to separate yourself from the chaos of intense emotions.

It strengthens emotional resilience, enabling you to handle life's ups and downs with greater composure and clarity. Instead of being swept away by emotions, mindfulness allows you to observe them, creating space for thoughtful responses rather than impulsive reactions. Through consistent practice, it equips you to manage stress and adversity with a sense of calm and perspective.

One of the most effective techniques for emotional regulation is mindful breathing, which acts as an anchor during turbulent moments. Imagine feeling a surge of anger or anxiety—your heart races, your thoughts spiral. In these moments, mindful breathing can be a lifeline. By focusing on each breath—slowly inhaling through the nose and exhaling through the mouth—you send a signal to your body to relax. This simple practice slows your heart rate, calms your mind, and creates a pause between emotion and action. Over time, practicing mindful breathing strengthens your ability to manage emotions effectively, preventing them from controlling your responses.

Another powerful technique is labeling your emotions, which can reduce their intensity and provide clarity. Often, emotions feel tangled and difficult to untwist. By identifying and naming them—whether frustration, sadness, or joy—you gain a clearer perspective. Labeling emotions creates psychological distance, helping you view them objectively rather than being consumed by them. This shift diminishes the emotion's power over you, allowing for more measured responses. Over time, this practice transforms how you experience emotions, turning them from overwhelming forces into manageable aspects of your inner world.

Developing emotional awareness is essential for effective emotional regulation. Mindfulness practices like journaling offer deep insights into emotional patterns. Writing about your feelings and experiences helps uncover recurring themes and triggers. This process enhances self-understanding, empowering you to address emotions constructively. Journaling is more than recording thoughts—it's a tool for self-discovery, revealing the underlying narratives that shape your emotional responses. Reflective meditation on emotions complements journaling by allowing you to sit with your feelings and explore them with curiosity. This practice nurtures self-compassion, encouraging you to embrace emotions without judgment.

Building emotional resilience is an ongoing process, strengthened through regular mindfulness practice. Each mindful moment reinforces your emotional coping mechanisms, preparing you to face challenges with confidence. Embracing emotional challenges with mindfulness means approaching them openly and seeing them as opportunities for growth rather than setbacks. This perspective transforms your relationship with emotions, fostering a sense of empowerment and self-assurance. As you cultivate resilience, you develop a set of strategies to draw upon in difficult times, ensuring you are equipped to handle whatever life brings your way.

Through mindfulness, you cultivate a deeper connection with yourself and develop greater control over your emotions. This practice empowers you to live with intention, responding to life's challenges with grace and strength. As you incorporate these techniques into your daily routine, your ability to regulate emotions expands, enhancing your well-being and enriching your relationships. With each breath and moment of awareness, you become more in tune with your inner world, learning to navigate its complexities with greater ease and understanding.

By embracing mindfulness for emotional balance, you lay the foundation for a more stable and fulfilling life. As this chapter concludes, it marks the beginning of deeper exploration and continued growth on your journey to resilience.

8

PERSONAL GROWTH AND EMPOWERMENT

P icture a sunflower in a garden. It begins as a tiny seed buried in the darkness of the soil. Over time, it pushes through the earth, reaching for the sun, growing taller and stronger each day. Personal growth mirrors this journey. It starts with recognizing the potential within yourself and nurturing it through life's challenges and triumphs. Growth is not a destination but a continuous process—a lifelong commitment to becoming the best version of yourself. It encompasses every aspect of your being—emotional, intellectual, and physical—each element influencing the others. Embracing personal growth means understanding that you are constantly evolving, learning from each experience, and adapting to change.

Personal growth involves recognizing opportunities for development in everyday life, often hidden within challenges and setbacks. These moments, though difficult, offer valuable lessons and the potential for transformation. Think about a time when a project at work didn't go as planned. Initially, it might have felt like a failure, but upon reflection, you likely uncovered key insights. Perhaps it strengthened your resilience or highlighted areas for improvement. Seeking feedback from colleagues can reveal further opportunities for growth, providing perspectives you might have overlooked. New experiences also serve as catalysts for development. Trying something unfamiliar —whether exploring a new hobby, stepping into a different role at work, or traveling to an unknown place—expands your comfort zone and enhances adaptability. Embracing these opportunities requires an open mind and the courage to step into the unknown, trusting that each experience shapes your progress.

Change, often feared or resisted, is one of the most powerful drivers of growth. Life transitions—starting a new job, moving to a different city, or entering a new relationship—present opportunities for transformation. Embracing change means viewing it not as a disruption but as a chance to evolve. It involves adjusting to new circumstances with flexibility and grace, recognizing that change is a constant part of life. By welcoming it, you allow yourself to grow, shedding old habits that no longer serve you and embracing new possibilities. This adaptability is essential for personal development, enabling you to handle life's uncertainties with confidence and resilience. Change should not be feared but embraced as an essential part of your journey, opening doors to fresh perspectives and new paths.

Celebrating milestones along the way reinforces the progress you've made. Reflecting on past achievements fosters a sense of accomplishment and motivation to keep moving forward. Consider keeping a personal growth journal—a space dedicated to documenting your journey. Use it to record significant experiences, insights gained, and goals achieved. This journal becomes a tangible record of your development, a reminder of how far you've come and what lies ahead. Acknowledging these milestones strengthens your commitment to personal growth, recognizing the effort and dedication it takes to reach them. It's a moment to pause, appreciate your journey, and honor the person you are becoming. Every milestone, no matter how small, is proof of your resilience and a stepping stone toward a more fulfilling life.

Interactive Element: Personal Growth Reflection Exercise

Take a moment to reflect on your journey of personal growth. Think about the challenges you've encountered and the lessons they've imparted. What milestones have you reached, and how have they shaped you? Capture these reflections in a personal growth journal, noting the areas where you aim to improve. This practice not only acknowledges your progress but also lays the groundwork for continued development.

As you move forward in your personal growth, remember that it is a lifelong journey requiring patience, curiosity, and unwavering self-belief. By identifying opportunities for growth, embracing change, and recognizing your achievements, you create a life filled with meaning and fulfillment. Personal development is not just about striving for more—it's about becoming your true self, aligning with your values and aspirations to live with purpose and joy.

Empowerment through Self-Awareness

Self-awareness is like a mirror reflecting the many facets of who you are—your strengths, weaknesses, and everything in between. It forms the foundation of personal empowerment, helping you make decisions that align with your true self. Recognizing your strengths allows you to apply them effectively in different areas of life, whether in your career, relationships, or personal pursuits. Perhaps you have a talent for problem-solving or a natural ability to empathize with and understand others. These qualities are your assets—tools that equip you to handle life's challenges. At the same time, acknowledging your weaknesses is just as important. It's not about dwelling on them but recognizing how they impact you and may be holding you back. This awareness allows you to address these areas, turning them from obstacles into opportunities for learning and growth. True empowerment comes from this balance—understanding where you excel and where you need support, enabling you to make informed and confident choices.

Enhancing self-awareness requires intentional practices that deepen your insight. Self-reflection exercises are a valuable starting point, encouraging you to pause and examine your thoughts, feelings, and actions. Setting aside time each day for reflection can help you gain clarity. Ask yourself questions such as, "What went well today?" or "How did I handle a difficult situation?" This habit fosters introspection, allowing you to recognize patterns and motivations that shape your experiences. Personality and behavior assessments can also provide additional insight. Tools like the Myers-Briggs Type Indicator (MBTI) or the Enneagram offer a structured way to explore your personality traits and tendencies. These assessments reveal aspects of your character that may not be immediately obvious, helping you understand how you interact with the world. By combining these methods, you cultivate a deeper understanding of yourself, creating a path for intentional living.

With greater self-awareness, you gain the ability to create meaningful change in your life. It begins with identifying areas for improvement —those aspects of yourself or your habits that you want to refine. This clarity allows you to set goals that align with your core values and aspirations. For instance, if you recognize a tendency to procrastinate, you can implement strategies to improve time management and productivity. If you notice a habit of avoiding difficult conversations, practicing assertive communication can help you build stronger and more open relationships. Self-awareness serves as a guiding force, helping you make choices that reflect your authentic self. It empowers you to align your actions with your values, leading to a more balanced and fulfilling life.

However, achieving self-awareness is not without challenges. One of the most significant hurdles is confronting uncomfortable truths about yourself. These realizations can trigger feelings of vulnerability or discomfort, often leading to a defensive response. Yet, facing these truths is essential for genuine self-awareness. It requires acknowledging aspects of yourself that you might otherwise ignore or suppress. Instead of viewing them as flaws, see them as parts of your human experience. Practicing self-compassion can help you accept these truths without self-judgment. Seeking honest feedback from others is also invaluable in this process. Friends, family, and colleagues can offer perspectives you may have overlooked, providing valuable insights into your behaviors and tendencies. Approach these conversations with an open mind, welcoming constructive feedback as a tool for self-discovery. By pushing past these barriers, you expand your understanding of yourself, unlocking new possibilities for growth and empowerment.

Setting Personal Goals for Change

Imagine standing at the edge of an open path, where each step you take shapes the direction ahead. Goal setting serves as a guide, leading you through personal and professional development. Goals act as milestones on this journey, providing clarity and purpose while turning aspirations into actionable steps. By defining what you aim to achieve, you transform vague dreams into concrete objectives, establishing a structured approach to progress. This clarity is essential, as it helps you focus your energy and resources on what truly matters, ensuring that each action is intentional and aligned with your vision.

Understanding the difference between short-term and long-term goals is key to creating an effective plan. Short-term goals are immediate steps, often achievable within weeks or months, providing quick wins that build momentum. These achievements boost motivation, reinforcing your commitment to long-term aspirations. In contrast, long-term goals represent the bigger picture, guiding your efforts over months or years. They demand patience and perseverance, as they involve significant change and personal growth. Striking a balance between short-term and long-term goals creates a flexible, sustainable strategy that keeps you focused while allowing room to celebrate progress along the way.

One practical approach to goal setting is adopting the SMART framework—Specific, Measurable, Achievable, Relevant, and Time-bound.

This method ensures that your goals are well-defined and realistic. Specific goals eliminate ambiguity, helping you concentrate on clear objectives. Measurable goals provide benchmarks to track progress and assess success. Ensuring goals are achievable allows you to set realistic expectations based on available resources and constraints. Relevance ensures that your goals align with your values and long-term vision, while time-bound goals introduce deadlines that create urgency and drive action. Applying this framework transforms aspirations into concrete, attainable plans, increasing the likelihood of success.

Developing a personal growth plan involves identifying key areas for improvement and establishing realistic timelines and milestones. Start by reflecting on aspects of your life you want to enhance, whether in your career, relationships, or self-improvement. Once you've identified these areas, set clear goals that incorporate both short-term and long-term objectives. Consider your current commitments and resources when setting timelines, ensuring that your goals are both challenging and achievable. Milestones act as checkpoints, allowing you to track progress, celebrate achievements, and reassess your direction if needed. This structured approach provides a solid foundation for growth, helping you navigate change with confidence and purpose.

Staying motivated and accountable is essential for reaching your goals, as the journey to change often includes obstacles and distractions. Regular goal reviews allow you to reflect on progress, recognize achievements, and make necessary adjustments. These reviews ensure that your goals remain relevant and aligned with your evolving aspirations. Establishing accountability through supportive relationships can further enhance this process. Whether through friends, family, or mentors, accountability partners help keep you on track by offering encouragement and constructive feedback. A structured support system reinforces motivation, builds resilience, and creates a sense of shared commitment. Consider setting up a shared calendar or scheduling regular check-ins with your accountability partner to discuss progress and address challenges. This collaborative approach strengthens focus and determination, making the journey toward growth more rewarding and sustainable.

In personal development, goal setting is more than a tool—it is a mindset. It represents a proactive approach to life, where you take charge of your future instead of merely accepting it. By defining clear and achievable goals, you assert control over your path, recognizing your ability to create meaningful change. This sense of empowerment builds confidence and fuels motivation, driving you to pursue your aspirations with determination. Ultimately, goal setting turns vision into reality, shaping a life filled with purpose, fulfillment, and success.

Building a Supportive Network

Imagine the comfort of knowing that, no matter what, you have people in your corner, ready to offer a helping hand or a listening ear. The power of a supportive network is a vital component in fostering personal growth. Emotional and practical support from a network of trusted individuals makes navigating life's challenges more manageable. When you face obstacles, having someone to lean on can provide security and encouragement. This network doesn't just offer support during tough times; it also enhances your overall well-being. Being part of a community uplifts your spirit, infusing your life with a sense of belonging and purpose. These connections enrich your life, creating a foundation of trust and solidarity that strengthens your resilience and empowers you to pursue your goals confidently.

Building and nurturing supportive relationships requires intentional effort and genuine interaction. To cultivate these connections, identify individuals who share your values and interests. These are the people with whom you can engage in meaningful interactions, forming deep and fulfilling bonds. Attend events or join groups that align with your passions, whether related to professional interests, hobbies, or personal growth. These settings offer opportunities to connect with like-minded individuals who can become part of your support system. Engage in conversations beyond surface-level topics, allowing you to understand and support each other openly. Such interactions foster mutual respect and empathy, creating a strong foundation for lasting friendships. By nurturing these relationships, you build a network that supports you and encourages your growth.

As you cultivate these supportive relationships, consider how to leverage your network for growth opportunities. Personal and professional networks are rich with potential for learning and development. Mentorship can be particularly transformative in leveraging your network. A mentor provides guidance and insight, sharing their experiences to help you navigate your journey. Seek out mentors who inspire you and whose expertise aligns with your aspirations. Their perspectives offer valuable lessons, providing new ways to approach challenges and decisions. Collaborative projects and learning experiences are also powerful opportunities for growth. By working with others on shared goals, you benefit from diverse perspectives and skills, expanding your understanding and capabilities. These collaborative efforts promote both personal and professional development while strengthening the bonds within your network, creating a cycle of mutual support and growth.

Building and maintaining a supportive network comes with its challenges. Social anxiety can be a significant barrier, making it difficult to initiate or strengthen connections. If you feel hesitant in social settings, start small. Attend smaller gatherings where interactions are more manageable, or bring a friend to ease the process. Practice active listening and show genuine curiosity—both can help reduce anxiety and encourage meaningful connections.

Another challenge is balancing the act of giving and receiving support. Relationships should be reciprocal, where both individuals feel valued and supported. Be mindful of opportunities to offer help and encouragement while also being open to receiving support when needed. This balance ensures that your network remains healthy and fulfilling, benefiting everyone involved. Although these challenges may take time and effort to overcome, doing so allows you to build a strong, supportive network that enriches your life.

As you reflect on the role of social support in your personal growth, consider ways to continue strengthening and expanding your network. Embrace the connections you already have while seeking opportunities to cultivate new ones. A supportive network provides more than just companionship—it strengthens you and fuels your drive to pursue your goals and aspirations. By surrounding yourself with people who inspire and uplift you, you create an environment where personal growth flourishes. These relationships form the foundation for future success, providing stability and encouragement as you navigate life's challenges. As you invest in and benefit from your network, you not only enhance your own growth but also contribute to the well-being and success of those around you.

9

OVERCOMING LONELINESS AND ISOLATION

I magine walking through a crowded city, surrounded by the hum of life yet feeling disconnected, as if moving through a muted world. The chatter of people, the laughter echoing from cafés, and the rush of daily life seem distant, like watching from behind a glass wall. This is the paradox of loneliness—a deep emotional void that lingers even in the presence of others. It is more than just being alone; it speaks to our fundamental need for connection. While solitude can be a chosen retreat for introspection and peace, loneliness is an emotional state where the absence of meaningful connection creates an overwhelming sense of emptiness. The lack of companionship and understanding can weigh heavily on the heart, making the world feel vast and unwelcoming.

For individuals with avoidant attachment, loneliness takes on a complex and challenging form. The very defense mechanisms designed to protect against emotional pain can, instead, reinforce isolation. Emotional withdrawal, a defining trait of avoidant attachment, builds an invisible wall between you and those around you. While this self-protective shell shields you from potential hurt, it also keeps genuine connection at a distance. This cycle of self-imposed isolation often stems from a fear of intimacy and vulnerability, leading to further withdrawal. What may feel like a safe harbor during uncertain times can, over time, erode the possibility of forming deep, meaningful relationships. The reluctance to seek support from friends or family is frequently driven by a fear of dependency or rejection. However, this hesitance only widens the gap, leaving you feeling unseen and disconnected.

Recognizing patterns of loneliness in your life is essential to breaking free from its grip. These patterns often emerge as a persistent sense of disconnection, where interactions feel surface-level and unfulfilling. You may avoid social settings, not from disinterest, but out of fear of exposing your vulnerabilities. This avoidance can also extend to family relationships, where expectations of emotional closeness feel overwhelming. Retreating into solitude may seem like the easier choice, offering an illusion of control and safety. However, this isolation often masks a deeper, unmet yearning for connection. The longer these patterns continue, the more ingrained they become, reinforcing the cycle of loneliness.

The effects of loneliness extend beyond emotional distress, significantly impacting mental and physical well-being. According to the CDC, a lack of social connection increases the risk of depression and anxiety, posing a serious threat to overall health. The emotional burden of isolation can lead to chronic stress, manifesting as fatigue, sleep disturbances, and stress-related illnesses. This prolonged state of high alert depletes the body's resilience, making it harder to cope with life's challenges. Loneliness can also contribute to feelings of hopelessness, where the future appears bleak and devoid of promise. It is a silent crisis that affects not only mental health but also physical vitality, diminishing one's ability to thrive.

Interactive Element: Loneliness Reflection Exercise

Take a moment to reflect on your experiences with loneliness. Think about the times you have felt disconnected or isolated. Write about these moments in a journal, noting any recurring patterns or triggers.

Consider how these experiences have affected your emotional and physical well-being. This exercise can reveal areas where change is needed, providing insight into steps you can take to build connections and reduce loneliness. Acknowledging these feelings opens the door to understanding and healing, paving the way for meaningful relationships and a true sense of belonging.

Strategies to Combat Isolation

Think about the times you've declined an invitation to a social gathering—not because you didn't want to go, but because the thought felt overwhelming. This is a common experience for those with avoidant attachment. Avoiding social events often becomes a protective pattern, shielding you from potential discomfort or judgment. Yet, this habit can lead to isolation, reinforcing loneliness over time. Recognizing this behavior is the first step toward change. A stream of negative self-talk often accompanies it, discouraging interaction. Thoughts like "I won't fit in" or "They won't miss me" become ingrained, shaping your social choices. While these thoughts may seem protective, they can confine you to solitude. Identifying these tendencies allows you to shift your perspective and take intentional steps toward connection rather than remaining stuck in fixed patterns.

Breaking free from isolation requires practical steps toward social engagement. Start small by setting achievable goals that gently expand your comfort zone. It could be as simple as greeting a neighbor or attending a local event. These small wins build confidence and gradually make social interactions feel more natural. Scheduling regular social activities can also be beneficial. Whether it's a weekly phone call with a friend or a monthly dinner with colleagues, planned interactions create opportunities for connection without the pressure of spontaneity. The key is consistency. By committing to these activities, you make social engagement a regular part of your life rather than an occasional effort. Over time, these interactions can shift from feeling like obligations to becoming a source of enjoyment and fulfillment.

Establishing a routine for social interaction is a powerful way to reduce isolation. Consider setting up weekly coffee meetups with friends. These casual gatherings provide a relaxed environment to strengthen relationships without the structure of a formal event. They offer a space to catch up, share experiences, and enjoy each other's company in a comfortable setting. Another option is joining clubs or groups that align with your interests. Whether it's a book club, hiking group, or cooking class, these spaces bring together people with shared passions, creating natural opportunities for connection. The focus on a common activity eases social pressure, making interactions feel organic and enjoyable.

The fear of rejection is a significant barrier to social engagement, often reinforcing isolation. It stems from the vulnerability of putting yourself out there and the possibility that your efforts may not be reciprocated. Cognitive-behavioral techniques can be effective in overcoming this fear. These strategies help you reframe negative thoughts, shifting from "What if they don't like me?" to "What if they do?" By challenging and modifying these internal narratives, you create space for positive experiences. Practicing resilience and self-compassion is equally important. Resilience means bouncing back from setbacks without allowing them to define your self-worth. It's about understanding that rejection is not a reflection of your value but a natural part of life. Self-compassion involves treating yourself with kindness and recognizing that everyone faces rejection at some point—it does not diminish your worth or potential for meaningful connections.

By applying these strategies consistently, you can break down the barriers of isolation, creating opportunities for meaningful connections and a more fulfilling social life.

Building Meaningful Connections

In a world that often values social media followers and online validation, the true essence of connection can be lost. It's not about the number of acquaintances you have but the depth of the relationships you build. Imagine a small circle of friends who know you inside and out—people you can call at any hour, who understand your quirks and stand by you through life's highs and lows. Developing a few close friendships like these can be far more fulfilling than maintaining a large network of superficial connections. Genuine relationships are built on meaningful interactions, where conversations go beyond the surface and focus on what truly matters. These friendships provide a sense of security and belonging, grounding you in an increasingly disconnected world.

Deepening relationships requires effort and intentionality. One effective approach is practicing active and empathetic listening. This means giving someone your full attention—truly hearing their words instead of planning your response while they speak. It involves acknowledging their feelings and validating their experiences, creating a safe space for open dialogue. Sharing personal stories is another powerful way to strengthen connections. When you open up about your own experiences, you invite others to do the same. This mutual exchange builds trust and deepens bonds, as people feel more connected to you and more comfortable sharing their own lives. Vulnerability becomes the bridge that fosters understanding and meaningful relationships.

Nurturing existing relationships is just as important as building new ones. Regular check-ins with loved ones—whether through a quick message or an extended conversation—help maintain the bonds you've already formed. These gestures show that you care about their well-being and value their presence in your life. Expressing appreciation and gratitude is another simple yet powerful way to strengthen relationships. A heartfelt thank-you or a small act of kindness can make someone feel valued and cherished. These moments remind others of their importance in your life, reinforcing the connection and encouraging mutual support. By prioritizing these relationships, you cultivate a strong support system that enriches your life and provides stability during challenging times.

Creating opportunities for connection often means stepping outside your comfort zone and seeking new experiences. Attending community events or workshops related to your interests can introduce you to like-minded individuals who share your passions. These gatherings offer a relaxed and engaging environment for meeting new people. Volunteering for causes that align with your values is another meaningful way to connect with others. It allows you to contribute to something greater while forming relationships based on shared goals and principles. These activities not only expand your social circle but also enhance your sense of purpose and fulfillment. They provide an opportunity to engage with the world in a way that leads to lasting and rewarding connections.

The Role of Community in Recovery

Being part of a community can feel like finding solid ground in a storm. It's a space where emotional support and validation thrive, offering a refuge where you can be yourself without fear of judgment. Imagine a group of individuals who understand your struggles, lending a listening ear and words of encouragement when you need them most. This is the power of community support—it fosters a sense of belonging and reassures you that you are not alone in your journey. In these spaces, shared experiences create deep understanding and empathy. You realize others have walked similar paths, and their stories resonate with yours, offering insight and hope. Communities also provide valuable resources, from advice on handling challenges to recommendations for professional help. The collective wisdom within these groups can uncover solutions and pathways to recovery that might otherwise remain unnoticed.

Finding the right community can be life-changing, aligning with your interests and values to create connections that feel genuine and meaningful. Online forums and support groups offer accessibility and convenience, allowing you to engage with others from the comfort of your home. These digital spaces serve as a lifeline, providing anonymity and safety as you share your thoughts and seek guidance. Local community centers and organizations, on the other hand, offer a more personal touch, encouraging face-to-face interactions that build trust and camaraderie. Whether it's a group centered on shared hobbies, mental health, or personal development, finding a community where you feel accepted and supported is essential. These spaces become a sanctuary where you can freely explore your thoughts and emotions, fostering emotional growth and resilience.

Contributing to community well-being can create a deep sense of connection and purpose. Participating in community service projects allows you to give back and make a meaningful impact on the lives of others. Whether volunteering at a local shelter, organizing a fundraising event, or joining environmental clean-up efforts, these activities connect you with like-minded individuals who share your passion for making a difference. Getting involved in community initiatives, such as hosting events or leading projects, strengthens your ties to the community. This engagement not only benefits others but also enhances your own sense of belonging, providing opportunities for personal growth and fulfillment. By actively contributing, you build relationships founded on trust and mutual respect, reinforcing the bonds that hold communities together.

Building a personal support network within a larger community requires intention and effort. Start by identifying individuals who share your values and interests. These people can serve as steady sources of support, offering guidance and companionship. Look for those who are empathetic, reliable, and open to meaningful, reciprocal relationships. Nurturing mutual support involves consistent communication and a commitment to being present for one another. It's about creating a network where everyone feels valued, and support is both given and received in a balanced, genuine way. This personal network becomes a safety net, providing both emotional and practical assistance when needed. Whether it's a friend who listens without judgment or a mentor who offers career advice, these connections serve as pillars of strength in your life, enhancing your well-being and resilience.

Reaching Out: Overcoming Barriers to Connection

Picture this: You are at a gathering, surrounded by familiar faces, yet you feel trapped by an invisible force of fear. This often stems from the fear of vulnerability and rejection—common barriers that prevent many from forming deeper connections. Vulnerability feels risky; opening up to others might lead to judgment or rejection. That fear can make you hold back, creating a shield to protect yourself. Social anxiety and self-doubt only add to the struggle. You may question your worth or worry about saying the wrong thing. These thoughts can be paralyzing, making it seem daunting to reach out.

Recognizing these barriers is the first step. It's about understanding that while these fears are valid, they don't have to control your actions. These challenges are not impossible to overcome—you can push past them with mindfulness and courage.

To break these barriers, start by initiating conversations with acquaintances. It may feel uncomfortable at first, but remember that most people appreciate a friendly gesture. Begin with simple topics—ask about their weekend plans or share a lighthearted story. These small interactions lay the foundation for deeper conversations and gradually build confidence in social settings.

Another effective strategy is to join activities that align with your interests. Whether it's a book club, a cooking class, or a sports team, these environments provide a natural way to interact with others. A shared activity eases the pressure of sustaining a conversation and offers common ground for connection. By engaging in activities you enjoy, you're more likely to meet people who share your interests, making it easier to form genuine relationships.

Practicing assertiveness in social interactions is another essential step in breaking down connection barriers. Assertiveness is not about being aggressive—it's about expressing your needs and boundaries clearly and respectfully. It involves communicating with confidence, using phrases like "I feel" or "I need" rather than hiding behind uncertainty.

To strengthen assertive communication, try role-playing social scenarios with a friend or in a supportive setting. This practice allows you to explore different responses and refine your ability to express yourself. It builds resilience, preparing you for real-life interactions. Over time, communicating your needs and setting boundaries will become second nature, allowing you to engage authentically with others.

Building confidence in social settings is a gradual process, but it's incredibly rewarding. One useful technique is role-playing different social scenarios. This helps you rehearse interactions, explore various ways to handle them, and ease your anxiety. Whether introducing yourself to a new group or joining an ongoing conversation, practicing these situations boosts your confidence.

Another helpful approach is gradually increasing your exposure to social situations. Start with smaller gatherings, then work your way up to larger events. Each experience builds on the last, improving your comfort and social skills. Confidence is like a muscle—it strengthens with consistent use. By gently pushing your limits, you develop the ability to navigate social settings with poise and assurance.

As you take these steps, remember that reaching out is an act of courage. It's about embracing vulnerability, not as a weakness but as a gateway to deeper, more fulfilling connections. With each effort, the barriers that once felt overwhelming begin to crumble. Embrace the process of building connections, knowing that meaningful relationships are waiting just beyond the walls of fear and doubt.

In this chapter, we've examined the challenges of overcoming barriers to connection, uncovering the fears that hold us back and the strategies that help us move forward. As you reflect on these insights, consider how they contribute to your personal growth and the depth of your relationships. The next chapter will build on this foundation, focusing on maintaining progress and developing secure, meaningful connections.

10

SUSTAINING PROGRESS AND
BUILDING SECURE RELATIONSHIPS

I magine a gardener tending to a delicate plant. They water it daily, adjust it to sunlight, and prune its leaves. Just like this plant, your emotional well-being requires consistent care and attention. You've embarked on a transformative journey, but maintaining that progress demands ongoing effort. The habits you've developed during your recovery from avoidant attachment are your tools—they are the water, sunlight, and care that nurture your growth and healing. Regular self-reflection sessions serve as your mirror, helping you recognize where adjustments are needed. These moments of introspection allow you to assess your feelings and reactions, ensuring you stay aligned with your goals. Additionally, consistently practicing mindfulness techniques keeps you grounded in the present, offering clarity and calm amid inevitable challenges. These practices don't just provide temporary relief; they become lifelong habits that support your emotional health.

Setbacks will happen—they are a natural part of any growth process. The key isn't to avoid them but to focus on how you respond. Developing a setback response plan can serve as your safety net, acting as a guide when you feel lost. This plan might include reaching out to an accountability partner who understands your journey and can offer support and perspective. A friend, mentor, or therapist can play this role, reminding you that you are not alone and helping you regain clarity when doubt clouds your thinking. With their support, you can view setbacks not as failures but as opportunities to learn and grow. This mindset shift is essential for sustaining change, enabling you to approach challenges with resilience and optimism.

Reinforcing positive changes in your behavior and mindset involves celebrating your achievements, no matter how small they may seem. Positive reinforcement can be a powerful motivator, whether it's treating yourself to something special after reaching a milestone or simply acknowledging your progress with gratitude. These celebrations serve as reminders of how far you've come, reinforcing the new patterns you've established. Over time, these small victories accumulate, building a foundation of confidence and self-assurance. Recognizing and celebrating your growth empowers you to keep moving forward, even when the path ahead feels daunting.

Continuous learning and adaptation are key to sustained progress. Engaging in personal development courses keeps you informed and inspired, offering new insights and perspectives that enhance your understanding of yourself and your relationships. Staying updated on research in attachment theory and related fields allows you to integrate the latest findings into your approach. This commitment to learning ensures that your growth remains dynamic, evolving to meet new challenges and circumstances. It's about embracing a mindset that welcomes change, recognizing every experience as an opportunity for further growth. By staying open to new knowledge and experiences, you create a life of continuous improvement, where each day brings fresh opportunities to nurture your emotional well-being.

Interactive Element: Setback Response Plan Template

Create a structured plan to handle setbacks effectively. Identify potential triggers, outline coping strategies, list contact details for your accountability partner, and include grounding activities that help you regain focus. Use this template to anticipate challenges and equip yourself with the necessary tools and support to stay on course. This plan serves as a proactive strategy for overcoming difficulties, reinforcing your dedication to growth and resilience.

The Path to Secure Attachment

Secure attachment functions like a well-balanced dance, where partners move in sync, guided by trust and openness. These relationships thrive on honest communication, allowing both partners to express their thoughts and emotions freely without fear of judgment. It's the ability to talk about a tough day at work or share dreams for the future without hesitation. This level of transparency creates an environment where misunderstandings are rare, and resolutions come with ease. Alongside communication, emotional stability plays a pivotal role. When challenges arise, those with secure attachment manage their feelings with composure, avoiding the emotional turbulence that often disrupts less secure bonds. This steadiness allows conflicts to become opportunities for growth rather than sources of division, strengthening the relationship.

Shifting from an avoidant attachment style to a secure one requires intention and effort. Someone making this transition might start by identifying role models who demonstrate secure attachment traits—friends, family members, or even colleagues who exude the calm confidence that comes with emotional security. Observing how they handle stress, communicate during disagreements, or express affection can offer valuable insights. Incorporating these behaviors into your own relationships can be a powerful tool for growth. Practicing secure attachment habits takes consistent effort and self-reflection. Prioritize being present with your partner, ensuring your interactions are genuine. When conflict arises, remain engaged rather than withdrawing. This active participation builds trust and reassures your partner of your commitment to the relationship's success.

Developing skills associated with secure attachment involves practical exercises that strengthen trust and emotional regulation. Trust-building activities with a partner can be as simple as setting aside dedicated time each week to connect without distractions. Use this time to share your highs and lows, listen actively, and express appreciation for each other's presence. These rituals reinforce trust, reminding both partners of the depth and value of their bond. Emotional regulation exercises, such as deep breathing or guided visualization, can help manage daily stress, allowing you to respond thoughtfully rather than react impulsively. Strengthening these skills fosters resilience, bringing stability and confidence to your relationships.

As you progress toward secure attachment, it's important to recognize and embrace your growth. Keeping a reflective journal can be a tangible way to track changes and celebrate milestones. Regularly writing about your experiences—how you navigate conflicts, express vulnerability, or strengthen connections—reinforces positive changes and highlights areas for further development. Constructive feedback from trusted relationships can also offer valuable insights. Encourage your partner or close friends to share observations about your behaviors and interactions. This feedback acts as a mirror, helping you see aspects of yourself that may not be immediately apparent. Welcoming both praise and constructive criticism deepens your self-awareness and supports your journey toward secure attachment. Through it all, be patient and kind to yourself. Growth is not always linear, and setbacks do not diminish your progress. Each step forward, no matter how small, is proof of your dedication to building secure, lasting relationships.

Long-Term Strategies for Relationship Success

Imagine an architect planning a building. Every line drawn and every material chosen reflects a vision of what that structure should be. Relationships, like buildings, require a blueprint—a clear vision that guides their formation and growth. Defining core relationship values lays the foundation for meaningful interactions. Perhaps honesty tops your list, ensuring open and transparent communication, even in difficult conversations. Maybe mutual respect is essential, allowing both partners to maintain their individuality while building a shared commitment. Once these values are established, setting relationship goals becomes the next step. These aspirations might include creating a supportive home environment, planning shared experiences, or committing to a weekly date night. These goals serve as milestones, marking progress and ensuring both partners move forward together. This clarity transforms the relationship from an abstract concept into a tangible and evolving bond.

The strength of a relationship depends on its ability to grow and adapt. Regular check-ins act as wellness assessments, helping partners address concerns before they become significant issues. These moments provide an opportunity to express needs, celebrate achievements, and resolve underlying tensions. Effective communication plays a crucial role in preventing and managing conflict. Addressing challenges early can stop them from escalating into full-blown disputes. A proactive approach emphasizes listening over talking and understanding over judgment. Techniques such as using "I" statements help frame discussions in a way that minimizes defensiveness and encourages open dialogue. This ongoing maintenance keeps the relationship dynamic, ensuring it remains a source of strength and support.

Relationships flourish when both partners are committed to personal and mutual growth. Sharing individual goals fosters alignment, ensuring both partners understand and support each other's aspirations. This sense of teamwork creates an environment where each person feels encouraged to pursue their dreams. Supporting each other might involve offering practical help or emotional encouragement during challenging times. A relationship built on shared growth enhances both partners' lives and strengthens their connection. It's about creating a space where both individuals thrive, knowing they have a steadfast ally by their side.

Emotional intimacy is the heartbeat of any relationship. Intentional efforts to nurture this connection can make all the difference. Engaging in shared activities, whether through hobbies or quiet evenings spent reflecting on the day, strengthens the bond between partners. The key is to create moments where both feel seen and heard. Open conversations about emotions provide a safe space for expressing feelings without fear of judgment. These conversations can be spontaneous, like nightly chats, or structured, such as monthly reflections on personal and relationship goals. Prioritizing emotional intimacy reinforces trust and security, ensuring the relationship remains fulfilling and resilient through life's inevitable ups and downs.

Celebrating Milestones in Personal Growth

Imagine standing at the peak of a mountain, looking back at the path you climbed. Each step represents a milestone in your personal growth, a reflection of the effort and determination you have invested. Recognizing these achievements is essential—not just for motivation but for acknowledging the progress you have made. Creating a personal achievement timeline can visually map your journey, marking significant moments and highlighting your growth. Whether digital or on paper, this timeline serves as a living record of your transformation, reminding you of your resilience and capability. Celebrating milestones with loved ones adds a communal element to your success, allowing you to share these moments with those who have supported you. These celebrations don't have to be elaborate; a simple gathering or dinner with friends can be a powerful affirmation of your progress.

Reflection is another vital component of personal growth, offering insight into your transformation. Writing reflective essays about your experiences provides an opportunity to explore the challenges you have faced, the lessons you have learned, and how you have evolved. Sharing these personal stories with peers reinforces your understanding and inspires those around you, creating a sense of connection and shared wisdom. This practice encourages ongoing introspection, deepening your awareness of your personal journey and continuous evolution.

As you celebrate achievements and reflect on progress, revisiting your goals and aspirations naturally follows. This process involves assessing where you are now and defining where you want to go next. Annual goal-setting retreats provide dedicated time and space for this reflection, helping you step away from daily distractions and focus on your objectives. During these retreats, you can refine your vision and values, ensuring they remain relevant and aligned with your evolving needs. Regularly revisiting and adjusting your goals keeps your path clear and your motivation strong, supporting ongoing development and maintaining a sense of purpose.

Gratitude plays a pivotal role in sustaining personal growth and well-being. Daily gratitude journaling fosters a mindset of appreciation, encouraging you to focus on the positive aspects of your life and recognize your progress. This practice shifts your perspective, helping you view challenges as opportunities for growth rather than setbacks. It strengthens emotional resilience and enhances overall satisfaction. Expressing gratitude to mentors and supporters further enriches this process, acknowledging the impact of those who have guided and encouraged you. This appreciation strengthens relationships and reinforces the connection between personal growth and collective support.

The journey of personal growth is ongoing, shaped by the milestones you achieve and the transformations you experience. By recognizing your accomplishments, reflecting on your journey, refining your goals, and embracing gratitude, you create a foundation for continuous self-improvement. This approach not only celebrates your progress but also prepares you for future challenges, ensuring you continue to evolve and thrive. In this way, personal growth becomes more than a goal—it becomes a way of life, where each step forward builds on the one before it, guiding you toward even greater achievements.

Looking Forward: A Life of Secure, Lasting Relationships

Imagine a future where relationships are built on security and trust, each connection reflecting growth and understanding. Envisioning this future begins with visualization exercises that bring clarity to your aspirations. Picture yourself in nurturing and supportive relationships where communication flows effortlessly and mutual respect forms the foundation. Consider crafting a personal relationship manifesto—a written declaration of the qualities and values you seek in your connections. This manifesto serves as a guide, keeping you aligned with what truly matters and leading you toward relationships that reflect your vision. It becomes a reflection of the future you desire, filled with trust, love, and empathy.

While dreaming of secure relationships, it's equally important to prepare for the inevitable challenges they may face. Anticipating potential obstacles allows you to develop strategies to address them effectively. Consider everyday hurdles such as communication breakdowns, differing priorities, or external pressures, and create action plans to overcome them. Strengthening resilience equips you with the tools to handle these challenges with confidence. This might include improving coping skills or seeking guidance from trusted advisors. By preparing for obstacles, you transform potential setbacks into opportunities for growth, reinforcing the foundation of your relationships.

Commitment to growth is essential for secure, lasting relationships. Setting long-term personal development goals that align with your relational aspirations provides direction and motivation. Engaging in continuous learning deepens your understanding of both yourself and your connections. Whether through workshops, reading, or interacting with diverse communities, expanding your knowledge fosters adaptability and growth. This commitment to learning ensures your relationships remain dynamic, fulfilling, and capable of evolving with time.

As you look ahead, consider embracing a relationship model rooted in security and mutual trust. This shift moves the focus from fear and uncertainty to collaboration and support. Surrounding yourself with like-minded individuals who share your values strengthens this commitment. Within this community, you find encouragement and accountability, reinforcing your dedication to secure relationships. Sharing your journey with partners and friends fosters a network of support, strengthening connections through shared experiences. Together, you explore new ways of relating, forging deep and enduring bonds. This collective approach enhances relationships, making them a source of strength and fulfillment.

By envisioning a future built on secure, lasting relationships, you lay the groundwork for a life enriched by meaningful connections. The path ahead holds limitless possibilities, each step guided by clarity, preparation, and a commitment to growth. As you embrace this new perspective, remember that the strength of your relationships lies in their ability to adapt and thrive. Your journey toward secure attachment reflects your resilience and capacity for love. Moving forward, let these principles guide you in creating a life where relationships are not just maintained but truly celebrated.

11

THE TRANSFORMATIVE POWER OF THERAPY

Therapy is a powerful tool for healing and personal growth, offering a structured space to explore your attachment style, overcome emotional barriers, and build healthier relationships. Whether you're addressing avoidant attachment or pursuing self-improvement, therapy provides the guidance and strategies needed for lasting transformation. However, it may not be the right fit for everyone. Some individuals find alternative approaches—such as self-help techniques, mindfulness practices, or support groups—more effective for their personal journey.

For those who choose therapy, it presents a unique opportunity to gain deeper insights, process emotions in a safe environment, and develop practical strategies for change. Working with a skilled therapist allows you to recognize patterns, strengthen resilience, and create a clear path toward a more secure and fulfilling life.

Interactive Element: Choose Your Path to Growth Therapy and self-help offer valuable paths to healing. Take a moment to reflect and determine what aligns best with your needs. Are you seeking professional guidance, personal reflection, or community support? Identifying what resonates with you is the first step toward meaningful growth. If therapy feels like the right choice, research professionals who specialize in attachment styles and emotional well-being. Prefer self-help? Begin with journaling or mindfulness practices to deepen self-awareness. Looking for connection? Consider joining a local or online support group to share experiences and gain encouragement.

Exploring the Roots of Attachment Styles and Therapy

Understanding the origins of avoidant attachment means: Examining childhood experiences is key to understanding the origins of avoidant attachment. Therapy provides a structured space to explore these influences and create lasting change.

Identifying Key Experiences: A therapist helps uncover formative events—such as emotional neglect or inconsistent caregiving—that contributed to your defense mechanisms.

Recognizing Patterns: Therapy highlights recurring behaviors, like avoiding vulnerability or mistrusting others, and offers strategies to break these cycles.

Processing Emotions: A safe environment allows you to reconnect with suppressed emotions and develop healthier emotional responses.

Providing Validation: Therapy reinforces that your feelings are valid and deserve recognition.

Psychodynamic and attachment-based therapies focus on how past experiences shape present behaviors, guiding you toward healing and emotional growth.

Therapy and Overcoming Emotional Barriers and Therapy

Avoidant attachment can make vulnerability challenging, but therapy provides a safe environment to practice openness and build trust. Several effective techniques can support this process:

Cognitive-Behavioral Therapy (CBT): This structured, evidence-based approach helps identify and challenge negative thought patterns. For example, you may believe, "If I rely on others, they'll disappoint me." A therapist guides you in reframing this belief into a healthier perspective, such as "Relying on others can build trust and connection." CBT also incorporates practical strategies like role-playing, thought journals, and gradual exposure to safe vulnerability, allowing you to rebuild trust in relationships over time.

Emotionally Focused Therapy (EFT): This approach centers on emotional bonds and is often used in couples therapy. It helps partners recognize and express their attachment needs while addressing patterns that create conflict. For example, a couple may struggle with one partner withdrawing emotionally while the other becomes more demanding. EFT helps both individuals communicate their deeper fears and needs, strengthening connection and trust.

These therapeutic methods break down emotional barriers, encourage deeper connections, and reduce feelings of isolation. They also provide practical tools to navigate vulnerability more effectively.

Building Trust, Healthy Relationships with Therapy

Therapy plays a vital role in rebuilding trust—both in yourself and in others.

Couples Therapy: This approach focuses on improving communication and resolving conflicts. Therapists help partners uncover underlying attachment dynamics and express their needs in a constructive way. For example, a therapist may guide a couple through active listening exercises, where each partner fully listens and validates the other's perspective. This practice strengthens trust and fosters a shared sense of security.

Individual Therapy: For those working through trust issues on their own, individual therapy provides a safe space to explore fears of intimacy and develop strategies for building trust. A therapist may help identify past experiences that contributed to mistrust and teach essential skills like boundary-setting and emotional regulation. These tools encourage confidence and openness in relationships.

By addressing the root causes of trust issues, these therapeutic approaches lay the groundwork for secure and fulfilling relationships.

Therapy and Developing Emotional Intelligence

Therapy plays a key role in enhancing emotional intelligence—the ability to recognize, understand, and manage emotions effectively.

Improves Self-Awareness: Therapy helps you identify emotional triggers and recurring patterns that may be holding you back.

Enhances Emotional Regulation: A therapist can introduce mindfulness techniques such as deep breathing and grounding exercises to help you manage overwhelming emotions with greater ease.

Strengthens Empathy: Exploring your own emotions in therapy deepens your ability to understand and connect with others, strengthening both personal and professional relationships.

By refining these emotional skills, therapy empowers you to navigate life with greater confidence, clarity, and emotional balance.

Therapy and Practical Tools for Transformation

Therapy provides actionable tools that support meaningful change, including:

Mindfulness Practices: Techniques such as mindful breathing help you stay present and manage stress effectively.

Somatic Therapy: Engaging with the body to release stored trauma and restore emotional balance.

Group Therapy: Building a sense of community through shared experiences, offering validation, and reducing feelings of isolation.

These therapeutic approaches complement self-help strategies like journaling and trust exercises, creating a well-rounded path to healing and growth.

Therapy and Personal Life Stories

Leah, a dedicated professional, struggled with avoidant attachment and found it difficult to delegate tasks. Therapy helped her challenge her fears of mistrust and practice letting go, leading to improvements in both her work and personal relationships.

Through Emotionally Focused Therapy (EFT), John and Marie rebuilt trust by exploring their emotional needs and deepening their connection through vulnerability. They learned to de-escalate conflicts and communicate more openly using structured exercises, transforming their relationship.

Keith, who exhibited avoidant attachment tendencies, frequently withdrew from close relationships to maintain emotional distance. In individual therapy, he uncovered the roots of his behavior, which stemmed from a childhood marked by inconsistent caregiving. Through attachment-based therapy, he gradually practiced opening up, learning to identify and express his emotional needs. Over time, he built deeper, more meaningful connections with friends and family.

As an entrepreneur with avoidant tendencies, Cathy struggled to collaborate with her team, fearing that delegating tasks would lead to failure. Through Cognitive-Behavioral Therapy (CBT), she recognized how past experiences with criticism contributed to her mistrust. Her therapist guided her in reframing these assumptions and practicing small, intentional acts of trust within her team. This shift not only strengthened her workplace relationships but also enhanced overall productivity and team morale.

If you feel stuck, therapy can help you move forward. Seeking support is a sign of strength and self-care. To find the right therapist:

Look for a specialist in attachment theory or relationship dynamics.

Use directories like Psychology Today or local mental health organizations.

Be open to exploring different therapeutic approaches.

Therapy provides a safe space to reflect on your past, address challenges, and build a path toward a more secure and fulfilling future. Whether through individual, couples, or group therapy, this support equips you with the tools and encouragement needed for lasting transformation.

Therapy is a powerful investment in yourself—an opportunity to heal, grow, and break free from the patterns that have held you back. Embrace it, and take the first step toward the life and relationships you deserve.

CONCLUSION

As you reach the final pages of this book, take a moment to reflect on your journey. Together, we have explored the complexities of avoidant attachment, uncovering the barriers that often hinder deep, meaningful connections. From understanding its origins and impact on relationships to discovering strategies for change, you have taken significant steps toward reclaiming your emotional freedom and building secure attachments.

This book has served as a guide on your path to healthier relationships. Through insights and practical tools, my goal has been to empower you to break free from the constraints of avoidant attachment. This journey is about embracing a life where intimacy is no longer a source of fear but a space of comfort and joy.

Take a moment to acknowledge your growth. Consider the progress you have made—whether recognizing patterns of avoidance, practicing emotional openness, or building trust with those around you. These are not small achievements. Each step forward is a testament to your courage and commitment to change. Celebrate these milestones, no matter how big or small. They are reminders of your transformation and the strength you have cultivated along the way.

Throughout this process, be kind to yourself. Self-compassion is essential as you continue developing emotionally. Treat yourself with the same patience and understanding that you would offer a dear friend. And when setbacks arise—as they inevitably will—view them as opportunities for learning rather than failures. Growth is not linear, but every effort you make contributes to lasting change.

Stay committed to your path. The progress you've made is only the beginning. With continued effort, you will experience even deeper transformations that enrich both your personal and relational life. As you move forward, maintain the habits and practices that have supported your growth. Let them serve as the foundation for a life filled with secure and lasting relationships.

Surround yourself with communities that uplift and support your journey. Whether through support groups, workshops, or connecting with like-minded individuals, these spaces provide encouragement and shared wisdom. They remind you that you are not alone and offer opportunities for mutual growth and understanding.

Put what you've learned into action. Set new personal and relational goals. Engage in activities that strengthen your connections with loved ones. Whether it's a weekly check-in with a partner or starting a new hobby with friends, these intentional actions reinforce the changes you have worked hard to achieve.

I extend my deepest gratitude for your dedication and openness to change. Your willingness to explore, challenge yourself, and embrace growth is truly inspiring. It has been an honor to walk this journey with you, sharing insights and strategies to help you thrive.

Envision a future where your relationships are built on security and trust, and emotional connections become sources of strength and joy. This vision is within reach. With continued commitment and self-compassion, you can create a life filled with meaningful relationships and personal fulfillment. Embrace this journey with hope and optimism, knowing that each step brings you closer to the life you deserve.

Thank You for Reading!

Your Review Can Make a Difference

Your story matters. Your experience with the Avoidant Attachment Recovery Solution can inspire and guide others on their path toward emotional freedom and meaningful connections.

Leaving a review isn't just about sharing your thoughts—it's about offering hope to someone searching for healing.

If this book has supported you in any way, I'd love to hear from you! Your words could be the encouragement someone else needs to begin their transformation.

Visit this link to leave your review:https://www.amazon.com/review/review-your-purchases/?asin=B0F3W448ZW

Thank you for being part of this journey.

With appreciation,

Luzivette Martinez

REFERENCES

A REVIEW OF ATTACHMENT THEORY IN THE CONTEXT. (n.d.). *National Center for Biotechnology Information.* Retrieved from https://pmc.ncbi.nlm.nih.gov/articles/PMC3051370/

Achieving a Healthy Work-Life Balance: Tips and Strategies. (n.d.). *Promise Care.* Retrieved from https://promisecare.com/achieving-a-healthy-work-life-balance-tips-and-strategies/

Avoidant Attachment in Adults at Work: Signs & Solutions. (n.d.). *Uncover Counseling.* Retrieved from https://uncovercounseling.com/blog/avoidant-attachment-in-adults-at-work/#:~:text=Avoidant%20attachment%20symptoms%20include%20a

BetterUp. (n.d.). How to Build Trust in the Workplace: 10 Effective Solutions. Retrieved from https://www.betterup.com/blog/how-to-build-trust

BetterUp. (n.d.). 12 Tips to Achieve and Maintain a Good Work-Life Balance. Retrieved from https://www.betterup.com/blog/how-to-have-good-work-life-balance

Bark. (2024). 2024 Gen Z Slang Guide For Dating and Relationships. Retrieved from https://www.bark.us/blog/genz-slang-dating/

CASE STUDY 6: 'Craig' and overcoming his avoidant attachment style. (n.d.). *CFC Living.* Retrieved from https://www.cfcliving.com/overcoming-avoidant-attachment-style/

Castrillon, C. (2023, March 12). Why Self-Awareness Is Essential For Career Success. *Forbes.* Retrieved from https://www.forbes.com/sites/carolinecastrillon/2023/03/12/why-self-awareness-is-essential-for-career-success/

Castrillon, C. (2023, December 17). 5 Powerful Strategies to Build Trust in the Workplace. *Forbes.* Retrieved from https://www.forbes.com/sites/carolinecastrillon/2023/12/17/5-powerful-ways-to-build-trust-in-the-workplace/

Dating Slang Terms - Your Ultimate Guide. (n.d.). *Zoosk.* Retrieved from https://www.zoosk.com/date-mix/dating-advice/dating-slang-terms-ultimate-guide/

Fearful Avoidant Attachment: What This Means in Relationships. (n.d.). *Healthline.* Retrieved from https://www.healthline.com/health/mental-health/fearful-avoidant-attachment#:~:text=People%20who%20develop

Finkel, D. (n.d.). Overcoming Delegation Anxiety. *Inc. Magazine.* Retrieved from https://www.inc.com/david-finkel/overcoming-delegation-anxiety.html

Gift Carnation. (n.d.). 40 Gen Z Slang Words & Relationship Lingo Explained. Retrieved from https://giftcarnation.com/blogs/gift-hamper/40-genz-slang-words-relationship-lingo-explained?srsltid=AfmBOoohg5OYIKmnwcoGRrTeb4IneIyL-HU8ed3wMxXgFkGxxIhtk_8aQ

How High-Performing Teams Build Trust. (2024, January). *Harvard Business Review.* Retrieved from https://hbr.org/2024/01/how-high-performing-teams-build-trust

How Leaders Can Build Psychological Safety at Work. (n.d.). *Center for Creative Leader-*

ship. Retrieved from https://www.ccl.org/articles/leading-effectively-articles/what-is-psychological-safety-at-work/

Kim, L. (n.d.). 10 Mindfulness Techniques to Practice at Work. *Inc. Magazine*. Retrieved from https://www.inc.com/larry-kim/10-mindfulness-techniques-to-practice-at-work.html

Loneliness, Lack of Social and Emotional Support. (2024). *Centers for Disease Control and Prevention (CDC)*. Retrieved from https://www.cdc.gov/mmwr/volumes/73/wr/mm7324a1.htm#:~:text=Loneliness

Mary Ainsworth Strange Situation Experiment. (n.d.). *Simply Psychology*. Retrieved from https://www.simplypsychology.org/mary-ainsworth.html

Mindfulness at Work: Cultivating Calm and Clarity. (n.d.). *Calm*. Retrieved from https://www.calm.com/blog/mindfulness-at-work#:~:text=Being%20mindful

Relaxation Techniques: Try These Steps to Lower Stress. (n.d.). *Mayo Clinic*. Retrieved from https://www.mayoclinic.org/healthy-lifestyle/stress-management/in-depth/relaxation-technique/art-20045368

Self-regulation tips for people with avoidant attachment style. (2023). *Hindustan Times*. Retrieved from https://www.hindustantimes.com/lifestyle/relationships/selfregulation-tips-for-people-with-avoidant-attachment-style-101692604982232.html

Simple Ways To Improve Students' Emotional Vocabulary. (n.d.). *The Reading Roundup*. Retrieved from https://thereadingroundup.com/emotional-vocabulary/

Snow HR. (n.d.). 20 Trust-Building Exercises and Activities for Teams. Retrieved from https://www.snowhr.com/BlogDetail/224/20-trust-building-exercises-and-activities-for-teams/0/all-categories

Synonyms for Irrational Fear of Intimacy. (n.d.). *Power Thesaurus*. Retrieved from https://www.powerthesaurus.org/irrational_fear_of_intimacy/synonyms

The 4 Best Meditation Apps of 2024. (2024). *The New York Times Wirecutter*. Retrieved from https://www.nytimes.com/wirecutter/reviews/best-meditation-apps/

The Words of Emotional Intelligence: Do's & Don'ts. (n.d.). *Cognitivus*. Retrieved from https://cognitivus.org/blog/emotional-intelligence-words-vocabulary

Your Thought Partner. (n.d.). How to Build Trust in the Workplace: The Ultimate Guide. Retrieved from https://www.yourthoughtpartner.com/blog/bid/59619/leaders-follow-these-6-steps-to-build-trust-with-employees-improve-how-you-re-perceived